Signs
of His
Coming

Signs of His Coming

DRAMAS & MEDITATIONS FOR ADVENT, CHRISTMAS, EPIPHANY

W. A. POOVEY

AUGSBURG PUBLISHING HOUSE
MINNEAPOLIS, MINNESOTA

SIGNS OF HIS COMING

NOTE: The dramas in this book are also available in a separate volume, *Signs of His Coming: Dramas*. No performance fee is required providing a copy of the play is purchased for each player.

MANUFACTURED IN THE UNITED STATES OF AMERICA

CONTENTS

"A" 2nd Adv

" C " 1st Adv

"B" 4th Adv.

"B"
6th Easter—

"A'
1st Sun of Kas

Christmas
Day
"B"

Preface

The Advent season is coming into its own again in the Christian church. There is also a revival of interest in the Epiphany season. Perhaps this renewed interest is to be expected. Worldly approaches to the celebration of Christmas have made the church realize it is extremely important that worshipers be led to the true meaning of Christ's coming.

The plays in this book seek to explore the various meanings of these special seasons. Dramas have a way of making clear certain truths whose meaning can be obscured by constant repetitions in sermons. This is not to say that sermons are old-fashioned or meaningless, but a change of pace can be useful in the worship life of a congregation.

The plays are largely contemporary, but run a gamut of types. The order of the Advent plays can be changed if desired and the Epiphany play may also be used for the Christmas celebration. All the plays are within the acting ability of the average congregation. They were originally presented at Holy Trinity Lutheran Church and St. John's Episcopal Church, both located in Dubuque.

The sermons are intended as guides for the pastor. In almost every instance the message of the play is clear enough that the sermon could be omitted.

However, many congregations are very sermon-oriented, and where this is the case, it might be unwise to present the play alone. This is a matter for each minister or worship committee to decide.

Plays involve the congregation in the worship service. They also involve people in work, and that isn't always popular. But if done well, plays like the ones in this book can be a powerful medium for presenting in a different way the age-old message of the gospel.

DRAMA

The Broom

MEDITATION

The Two Faces of John the Baptist

The Broom

CHARACTERS

HELEN: young wife

FRANK: Helen's husband

KAREN: a friend

JOHN: the street cleaner

MR. DARBIN: official, stern

MRS. LALU: fussy, mannish in dress

MR. BAGUM: same type as Darbin

CROWD: as many other characters as will fit on the stage

SETTING

Open stage. The characters line one side of the street, facing audience. JOHN should not be forced to turn back on audience, so the line must be broken at times. Contemporary costumes.

11

The Broom

As the play opens, a READER *may read Matthew 3:1-10 although this isn't necessary. Then the crowd comes down the aisles and takes their places in the chancel. As they come they sing the following song, repeated once or twice as necessary:*

W. P.

W. A. Poovey

We are wait-ing for the king, Wait-ing for the king, Wait-ing for the king all

day. We are look-ing for the king, Look-ing for the king,

Look-ing for the king to lead his peo-ple. We are sing-ing our song,

Sing-ing our song, Sing-ing our song all day. We are prais-ing his name,

Prais - ing his name, Prais - ing his name For he's our lead - er.

The crowd take their place and jockey for position. KAREN who has entered with the crowd keeps a space around her. DARBIN, LALU and BAGUM stand together on opposite side of stage. Then HELEN and FRANK come hurrying down the aisle.

HELEN: Do you think it will be today? Will the king come today?

FRANK: How should I know? People have been expecting him for a long time, and he hasn't showed up yet.

HELEN: What are we hurrying for then?

FRANK: Because everyone else is. Besides, there are some rumors in the city. But you can't expect a king to appear on schedule. You just have to wait until he thinks it's the right time for him to come.

HELEN: I suppose that's so. *(Sees KAREN.)* Oh, there's Karen. She's probably got a place for us. I told her to try to keep some free space if she got here first. *(Shouting.)* Karen, Karen.

KAREN: Come on. *(They hurry onstage.)* I've been keeping this spot but I can't hold out much longer. The crowd is getting denser all the time.

HELEN: We've been hurrying. But we got a late start.

FRANK: It's probably hurry up and wait. *(They crowd in.)*

HELEN: Thanks, Karen. This is a good place.

FRANK: Yeah, thanks.

KAREN: I'm so glad you got here. There's a big crowd

today. There's even a delegation from City Hall. So maybe this is the right day.

FRANK: From City Hall, eh? They must know something.

HELEN: Oh how thrilling it would be if the king did come along today. I think I would just die from excitement.

FRANK: You'd better go home right away, then.

HELEN: Oh, you know what I mean. *(Faint noise in distance which gets louder and louder. Noises can be recorded or made by people off stage.)*

KAREN: Listen. I think I hear something. It sounds like cheering.

FRANK: Cheering! It sounds more like people laughing.

HELEN: Laughing? *(Crowd pushes forward.)*

FRANK: Yes, laughing. But would they be laughing at a king?

KAREN: Stop pushing

FRANK: Yeah. Stand back so we all can see. *(Laughter gets stronger.* JOHN *enters, sweeping the street.)*

HELEN: Oh, for goodness sake. It isn't the king at all. It's only old John, the streetcleaner.

FRANK: No wonder they're laughing. Here he comes with his shabby pushbroom. *(Calling)* Hello, John. Looks like your business is cleaning up, eh? *(Laughs.* CROWD *groans.)*

JOHN: That's only the 75th time I've heard that joke today.

HELEN: I guess that'll hold you, Frank. But John, is the king coming? Is this the day?

JOHN: This is the day. Or just like the day. The king is coming soon. That's why I'm sweeping the streets.

FRANK: You've got a useless job. The streets will just get dirty again.

JOHN: I know that. But you can't expect a king to come riding along a dirty street. Every street in the city must be swept. Every corner must be cleaned. For the king sees everything. His eyes pierce into the darkest holes. So I have to get things cleaned up for him. (KAREN *drops a kleenex.*) Here you. Pick that up.

KAREN: I'm sorry. I didn't think.

JOHN: Well, you'd better think. Everyone must think. There mustn't be any trash on the road, any dirt on the path when the king comes.

FRANK: The way you talk, he must be some king.

JOHN: He's the only king there is. And he's coming from his palace above to visit his people. We've all got to be ready for him. (To HELEN) But you're not ready.

HELEN: Of course I am. I've been up since dawn, and I hurried like mad to get here on time. I'm all excited just at the thought of the king's coming.

JOHN: But you're not ready, you've got a dirty smudge on your face.

HELEN: I have! Is he telling me the truth, Frank?

FRANK: He sure is. Your face *is* dirty. I told you to wash before we left.

HELEN: I was in a hurry. There wasn't time for everything.

JOHN: Clean up, clean up for the king.

FRANK: That's telling her, John.

JOHN: Don't you talk, fellow. You're not ready for the king either.

FRANK: What's the matter with me?

JOHN: You've got a rip in your trousers. See. See.

FRANK: Say, I believe you're right.

HELEN: He is right.

FRANK: Well, if you'd tend to your sewing.

HELEN: Just like a man. Blaming me.

FRANK: I'll stand behind you and Karen. That should cover up the tear.

JOHN: Mend the tear. Mend the tear. Don't just cover it up. Everything must be right for the king.

KAREN: John, what must I do to be ready for the king? Tell me, tell me.

JOHN: You look pretty good to me. (*Looking closely at her.*) I have it. You look too serious. You need to smile, not frown. The king wants his people to be happy. He brings a message of good news to those who are ready for him. Smile, not frown!

KAREN: Smile, not frown. Smile, not frown. I'll try to remember.

JOHN: You do that. (*To others in the* CROWD.) That goes for you too. Smile, not frown. Straighten up. Don't shove others. Everyone must be ready when the king comes. And I have to get on with my sweeping.

(*He sweeps for a while. The* CROWD *straightens up and then begins to sing the song again and sings it once or twice.* JOHN *moves down to where the delegation stands, silent, not participating.*)

JOHN (*seeing the delegation*): Aha! I recognize you three. You're from City Hall.

DARBIN (*harshly*): And why not? We have a right to be here. I might even say we have a duty to be present.

MRS. LALU: That's right. We're here to welcome the king and to rejoice in his coming.

JOHN: Nonsense! You don't intend to do anything of the kind.

MR. BAGUM: Why do you say that?

JOHN: Because you represent the rulers here. And when the king comes, *he* will be the ruler. You don't want him to come. You don't love him. You love your possessions and your power. But don't think just because you have been in charge for so long that you'll be protected from the king's wrath. You can't fool him. He sees and knows what's in a man's heart. Take my broom and clean out the dirty places in your hearts if you want to be received by the king.

MR. BAGUM: Now wait a minute. You're a very insolent street cleaner. (MR. DARBIN *pulls him aside and whispers in his ear.*) Say, you're not the king himself, travelling in disguise, are you?

JOHN: What a silly question!

MR. BAGUM: Well, answer it.

JOHN: I am not the king.

MRS. LALU: I've just had a thought. Are you the king's chief advisor?

JOHN: I am not.

MR. DARBIN: Let me try. Tell me, you noisy street cleaner. Are you the king's spy, sent to check up on us?

JOHN: No!

MRS. LALU: Well, for goodness sake, who are you? What right have you to go around telling people what they should do? I've got to give them a report down at City Hall when I get back. Who do you claim to be?

JOHN: Nobody. Nobody at all. I'm just the street sweeper. Nobody notices me. I'm just a broom, just a dustpan. But I have a job from the king. I have to sweep the streets, clean the city, make everything ready for him. And I'm calling out to all of you, get ready for his coming. Sweep out your hearts. Clean your minds. Drive out the dust and sweep out the cobwebs. For the king will come. He is near, very near to all of us.

FRANK: But what will he do when he comes, John? What will things be like then?

KAREN: Yes, tell us, John. Tell us.

JOHN: You'll see, you'll see when he comes. He'll make this city a great city of shining buildings and pleasant parks. The very streets will be paved with gold. The king will rule in the city, he will rule all people with love and justice. There will be no place for evil here, no room for hypocrisies and plots. The evil will be gone and only the good will remain. Only those who have learned the meaning of love will remain in this city. So prepare your hearts, all you people. The king is coming. The king is near.

(Trumpets sound off stage. These can be recorded on tape or played by a musician.)

ALL: The king. The king. He's here. The king. *(They all rush off stage.)*

JOHN *(leaning on broom):* Now it's in his hands. And I can get on with my cleaning. *(He sweeps off stage. Lights or music indicate the end of the play.)*

The Two Faces of John the Baptist

Text: Matthew 3:1-10

Strange! Paradoxical! Far-out! Those are some of the terms which describe John the Baptist. His story seems almost unbelievable to our modern ears, and he must have been an "odd-ball" even to the people of his day. He was flamboyant, a character. His message, his mode of dress, even his diet was startling. On the other hand John seemed at times modest and retiring. He claimed no position of importance for himself, insisting that he was only a voice crying in the wilderness. He directed his own disciples to Jesus, declaring: "He must increase, I must decrease." One almost feels that John was a split personality, a good case for a psychiatrist.

Yet it is John's message, not his person, that is important for us today. What he said can still guide men in the twentieth century. But the words of John exhibit this same kind of divided stress, the same mixture of hardness and softness, of denunciation and invitation. To paraphrase a movie title, we need to observe *The Two Faces of John the Baptist,* if we would understand him.

It is certainly obvious that John's message had its hard side. How would you feel if the minister stood in the pulpit on Sunday morning and called some of the congregation "snakes"? That is the language of John, "brood of vipers." Not a very pleasant greeting, particularly to men who were used to receiving the deference and respect of others. Even John's call for repentance is a stern one, for repentance implies that a man has been going in the wrong direction and needs to turn around. Indeed we might sum up John's message by the simple statement, "You can't fool God. You can't play games with the Almighty." John in the strongest kind of language called on men to be honest, to stop pretending that they were more holy than they really were. Men must turn around and change their way of living.

But John is not alone in making such demands. This hard-driving type of language appears again and again in the Bible. Isaiah pictures God as repudiating the worship and the prayers of the people because they have not repented of their sins. Jeremiah spoke so sternly to the leaders of his day that they threw him into a pit so they wouldn't have to listen to him any more. The author of the last book of the Old Testament describes God accusing his people of robbing him and of oppressing the poor.

Nor is this kind of language foreign to Jesus, whom we usually picture as presenting a message of love and peace. Jesus, like John, began his ministry with a call to repentance. Later Jesus called down punishment on some of the cities that failed to be moved by his miracles. Jesus matched John in the harsh-

ness of his language when he called some of the
leaders "whitewashed tombs, full of dead men's
bones." The gentle Jesus had his moments of stern-
ness when the occasion demanded such a response.
The call for absolute honesty, for repudiation of all
that is evil and false, rings from every page of scripture.

There is no doubt that we live in a softer age.
Men do not like to be told about their sins today,
and all too often ministers are tempted to speak
only what congregations want to hear. Excuses are
found for almost every weakness of human nature.
We are the products of our environment or the vic-
tims of heredity. When all else fails situational ethics
seems to be able to find an excuse for almost any
action so long as we insist that it proceeded from
"love." Too often God is thought of, not as a concerned Father but as a senile grandpa who indulges
his grandchildren or ignores them when they are
naughty. One of the verses from *The Rubaiyat* ex-
presses this lackadaisical attitude very well:

> Some there are who tell
> Of one who threatens he will toss to Hell,
> The luckless pots he marr'd in making, pish,
> He's a good fellow and 'twill all be well.

In the face of such an attitude, the message of
John the Baptist is a timely one. He still calls on
men to repent. He says we cannot fool God; we
cannot sweep under the carpet the dirt in our lives.
We must face honestly the failures of our daily conduct and must reckon with the presence of a righ-
teous God in this universe. To put it on a very per-

sonal level, suppose the street cleaner in our play stood before you. What would he say? What would he ask you to sweep out of your life so that you might be ready for the coming of the King? I do not know what his message would be to you, but all of us would prove to have some flaws.

Today is a day to think about that. For the Advent season is a time for street cleaning, for cleaning out the streets and the alleys and back lanes of the heart. The message still rings clear. Repent. Repent.

But we are considering the *two* faces of John the Baptist. And the other face is equally important. Too often John is thought of as an Old Testament prophet of the law who has somehow wandered into the New Testament world by mistake. Such a view is terribly misleading. John doesn't call for repentance because he seeks to improve the general conduct of human beings. John announces the coming of a King. He isn't just a fussy street cleaner who hates to see dirt lying around in the city. John is a herald, an announcer of good news.

Somehow, no matter how many times we say it, people forget that the gospel is good news. We tend to forget that there is purpose behind all the stress on sin and repentance in the Bible. Underlying everything else is the message that we have a shepherd, a King, a Savior. God calls us to repentance only in order to prepare us for blessing and peace. Note how often the motif of joy appears in the New Testament. We are guests at a wedding. We are people invited to a feast. We are people who have found a pearl of great price or a treasure hidden in a field. Joy, joy, joy is the message of the gospel.

That very fact should make us revise our picture

of John the Baptist. He is usually pictured as a stone-faced prophet who thundered his message at people and roared at them because of their sins. I don't believe he was like that at all. John must have been a man who exulted in the good news that he was sent to proclaim. His face must have shone with joy as he cried to Israel that the long-awaited king was about to appear.

We need to experience that same exultation in the Advent season. Too many think of Christianity as a religion that deprives men of the pleasures and enjoyment of life. The words *puritan* and *blue-nose* seem to equal *Christian* in the minds of many. But that's all wrong. Christians turn away from evil because they have something better in life. We have a king, a Lord and Savior to give us joy even in the midst of the ugliness of this world.

The exulting remarks of the street cleaner at the end of the play are not paralleled by any actual words of John. Yet the picture of a city of God where love and justice dwell is not an idealistic picture but is precisely the vision conjured up by John's announcement of the coming of the Messiah. We still look toward that city.

Thus the two faces of John the Baptist form one picture. The call to repentance is a necessary part of the summons to a new life in Christ. The believer must seek again and again to sweep away the dirt of sin and evil in his life. He does this at Advent and at Lent and in a sense every day. But he does this because he is looking forward to something better, something more glorious. The King has come and is always coming into our hearts.

Admittedly this call to a better life is sometimes

hard to accept. We have to let go of our old ways, let loose of our old sins, if we would receive the blessings of the kingdom.

This reminds me of the time a friend invited me to go for a sail on Lake Michigan. When I looked at the size of the boat and the size of the lake, I didn't want to leave the shore. Then someone picked me up and dropped me in the boat, and in a few minutes I was enjoying a beautiful sail in the moonlight.

In a similar way we sometimes cling tenaciously to our present sinful life. But the message of Advent is simple. Let loose. Let loose of everything that holds you back. Trust your life to the King. Trust the one whose coming was announced by that strange man John the Baptist. You will never be disappointed.

SECOND SUNDAY IN ADVENT
LUKE 21:25-27

DRAMA

The Wreath

MEDITATION

Jesus Is Best

The Wreath

CHARACTERS

    HENRY FREDERICKS: middle-aged, a bit stubborn but a good Christian father

    BLANCHE FREDERICKS: same age as husband, a little more lively

    KATHIE FREDERICKS: teen-ager, serious, argumentative

    PHIL FREDERICKS: about 12, mischievous, fun-loving

SETTING

    Possibly a dining room with the family seated around the table. An Advent wreath with the candles burning is in the center of the table. The family has just finished a devotional reading from a booklet and are ready for the prayer as the play begins.

HENRY *(handing booklet to* KATHIE*)*: That's the Advent reading for tonight. Now Kathie, suppose you read the prayer and then Phil can blow out the candles.

PHIL: O.K. Dad. *(Pause.)*

BLANCHE: Go ahead, Kathie.

KATHIE *(has been looking at booklet)*: No. No, I won't do it.

HENRY: You won't do it! Well, why not, for goodness sake? Our family always take turns reading the prayer at the end of our devotions. You know that.

KATHIE: Yes, I know. And I always like it when it's my turn. But not tonight. Not this prayer. I won't pray it.

HENRY: Don't be so stubborn. Just read the prayer the way it's printed.

BLANCHE: Now wait a minute, dear. There must be something wrong. What's the matter with the prayer, Kathie?

KATHIE: Well, it's about the second coming of Christ.

BLANCHE: Yes, in the Advent season we think about Christ's return as well as his first appearance here on earth.

PHIL: Even I know that.

HENRY: Sure. What's wrong with a prayer about Christ's second coming?

KATHIE: There's nothing wrong with it. But the

prayer in this booklet says, "Lord Jesus, come quickly." And I don't want him to come quickly, I'm not going to pray a prayer that says something I can't agree with.

HENRY: Why are you kicking up such a fuss? Christians have always hoped and prayed that the Lord would return. They've been doing that for almost 2000 years. Why are you suddenly getting excited?

KATHIE: It's very simple. I don't want the Lord to come back. Not now, not in my lifetime. At least not as long as I'm able to live and enjoy things.

BLANCHE: What makes you say that, Kathie?

PHIL: She's talkin' kinda crazy. I'd get a spanking if I talked like that. Wouldn't I, Dad?

KATHIE *(disgusted):* Oh, Phil. *(Turns to others.)* It's just that I haven't really had a chance to live. And if Jesus comes back soon, I won't ever get that chance.

BLANCHE: What do you mean, dear?

KATHIE: Well, look, I'm only in high school. Next year I plan to go to college. Then one day I—well, I hope to get married and maybe have a family of my own. But if the world ends soon, I won't get to do any of those things.

PHIL *(excited):* Say, if that happened, I wouldn't get to try out for the baseball team next year. I'm on Kathie's side.

HENRY: You two silly kids. Putting baseball and marriage ahead of the second coming of Christ.

KATHIE: It's easy for you to talk. You and Mother have lived your lives but Phil and I are just getting started.

BLANCHE: Well, thanks a lot. But I'm really not ready for my social security yet.

KATHIE: I didn't mean that you were. I guess I'm not making myself clear. I know the world is going to end someday. Maybe it will happen tonight. But I'm not going to be glad about it or pray that God will hurry up and put a stop to things the way they are now. And I don't really think many other people want to pray a prayer like that.

HENRY: But Kathie, you're contradicting everything that Christians believe. Here, hand me my Bible from the table over there. (PHIL *gets the Bible.* HENRY *looks through it.*) I know it's here. Yes, at the very end. Listen to this from the Book of Revelation. "He who testifies to these things says, 'Surely I am coming soon.'" That's Jesus talking, and then John answers, "Amen. Come, Lord Jesus." See. That's the way a Christian should feel about the second coming.

PHIL: Well, what have you got to say to that?

KATHIE: I don't want to quarrel, Daddy. But I think that's the way John felt because he was a prisoner on an island or something. I don't blame him for wanting the world to come to an end if he was suffering. But I'm not a prisoner. I'm enjoying life. That's different.

BLANCHE: She's right about that, Henry. Most of the people in the Bible who talked about the second coming were having a pretty rough time of it. They were being hated or persecuted because of their faith. No wonder they wanted the world to end in a hurry.

HENRY: Are you going to turn against me too?

PHIL: Hurray! That makes three of us against the second coming.

HENRY: Oh, for heaven's sake. Doesn't the Bible mean anything to you young people? You're so silly about the truth these days.

KATHIE *(stung):* I knew you'd say that. You think a person can't have any different ideas than you do. But I'm not just being silly. I think Christian people ought to be happy with the world we live in now. Why should we act like we want everything to end?

HENRY: Look, there are people who are sick and people who are old and some who are handicapped. Can't you see that the second coming will put an end to all those evils? We ought to want it to happen for their sake, at least.

KATHIE: Daddy, I'm not saying things are perfect now. And I'm sorry for people who are suffering. I just want the same chance as you had to grow up and live my life the way it should be lived.

PHIL: And I want a chance to make that baseball team next spring.

HENRY: Look, we've wasted enough time. Saying a prayer about Christ's coming won't make that

much difference. The end of the world is probably
a long way off anyway.

KATHIE: Then I don't see any sense in praying such
a prayer. *(The phone rings offstage. This can be
done by using a tape recording or a bicycle bell.)*

BLANCHE: There's the phone. I'll get it. You three
argue this thing out while I chat.

HENRY: Always the phone. It'll probably ring right
in the midst of the second coming and this family
will be late for all the excitement because we won't
want to miss a phone call.

KATHIE *(shocked):* Oh Daddy!

HENRY: Just joshing you a bit. But Kathie, there
must be a reason why Christians have always
prayed for Jesus to return and have wanted him
to come quickly.

KATHIE: I told you the reason. Christians were always
having a bad time of it. And Christ's return would
get them out of a tight fix.

HENRY: Do you really think that was all that made
them feel the way they did?

KATHIE: I'm sure. The end of the world is a comfort-
ing thing if you're having a rough time.

PHIL: Say, maybe that's the way to get out of that
old math test I have next Monday. Maybe you
ought to say that prayer, Kathie, if you think it will
work.

KATHIE: Phil, you're impossible. But Daddy, I don't

think people should be expected to pray for the
second coming if they're enjoying themselves.

HENRY: Maybe that's the trouble with Christians today. They're having too good a time. They ought
to suffer more. Then they wouldn't talk like you
do.

PHIL: Say, are you going to suffer, Dad? What are
you going to do? Sell the car and walk to work?

HENRY: Don't be impertinent, young man.

KATHIE *(pressing her advantage):* You see? Nobody
wants to lose what he has, not even you. And
why should we? Doesn't God bless us and provide
us with the comforts that we have?

HENRY *(retreating):* I suppose so.

PHIL: We're always thanking him for things. You
did tonight when you said grace before dinner.

KATHIE: Sure you did. And I don't see anything
wrong with our enjoying the good things that God
gives. Is it wrong, Daddy?

HENRY *(aware he is being beaten):* No, I don't suppose so.

KATHIE: Well then, why should we want those good
things to come to an end right away? Why should
I pray for the second coming and the end of the
world?

HENRY: There's something wrong in all of this, but
I don't seem to be able to put my finger on the
weak spot.

PHIL: Maybe you just don't want to admit that you're wrong and Kathie is right for once.

KATHIE: This will be the first argument I've won in a long while.

HENRY: You haven't won this one yet. The whole church can't be wrong, and my daughter Kathie be right. It doesn't make sense.

KATHIE (*sensing victory*): But you won't make me read that prayer tonight will you?

HENRY: No, I won't do that. (BLANCHE *reenters.*) Oh, here comes your mother now.

BLANCHE: Well, that was some call. Before I hear how your argument came out, I have some wonderful news. Guess who that was on the phone?

PHIL: The President of the United States?

HENRY: Phil! Blanche, why don't you tell us and then we'll all know.

BLANCHE: It was Aunt Alma.

ALL: Aunt Alma!

BLANCHE: Yes. And she's coming to visit us.

HENRY: Say, that's good news. She's the only relative on your side of the family that I enjoy having here.

PHIL: When is she coming? Boy, she always brings me a present.

BLANCHE: Phil! That's not the right attitude.

PHIL: Oh, I'll be glad to see Aunt Alma even if she doesn't bring me anything. I *like* her.

KATHIE: Will you stop chattering about presents so Mother can tell us when Aunt Alma is coming?

BLANCHE: She's coming tomorrow. She's driving through town with some friends, and they expect to spend tomorrow afternoon and evening here, so Aunt Alma will come out and pay us a visit while they're in town.

HENRY: Tomorrow afternoon, eh?

BLANCHE: Yes. I was supposed to go to a show for Mildred Johnson, but I'll call and excuse myself.

HENRY: Say, I'll have to cancel my golf date with Ray Ellison. He's been wanting to play golf with me for a long time. But Aunt Alma comes first. I suppose you two kids will be busy as usual on Saturday afternoon?

PHIL: Not me. I was going to a show with Jimmie, but I'm not going to miss out when Aunt Alma is here.

KATHIE: I had plans too, but I'll phone Dotty and tell her we'll go shopping some other day. Oh— (*An idea has struck her.*)

BLANCHE: What's the matter?

KATHIE: Nothing. I just thought of something, that's all.

BLANCHE: Well, it's nice that we can all be here when Aunt Alma comes. I'm so glad she can come. But now tell me, who won the argument about the prayer?

HENRY: Surprisingly enough, Kathie won. I promised she didn't have to read that prayer about the second coming. I guess we'll have to use another prayer tonight.

KATHIE: That won't be necessary now. I'm ready to read the one in our devotional book.

HENRY: What! You argue your head off and almost convince me you're right and I'm wrong. And now you say you're ready to read the prayer. What kind of a game are you playing?

KATHIE: No game. It's just that suddenly—suddenly I've changed my mind.

HENRY: And who changed it for you?

KATHIE: Nobody. Well, maybe Aunt Alma.

HENRY: Aunt Alma! Say, you're talking crazier now than you did before.

KATHIE: Are you all ready for the prayer?

BLANCHE: I am, and I think I understand what happened, Kathie, to make you change your mind.

PHIL: I'm ready. I've been ready to blow out the candles for hours.

HENRY (*angry and mystified*): Well, I'm not ready. And I won't be ready until somebody tells me what's going on. Aunt Alma and the second coming. What next?

KATHIE: It's very simple, Daddy. When we heard that Aunt Alma was coming, we all changed our plans. You gave up your golf game, and Mother decided to stay home from the shower, and Phil called off his trip to the movies, and I decided to forget about going shopping with Dotty.

HENRY: Yes? So what?

KATHIE: We gave them up because we wanted to be with Aunt Alma. We all love her. Suddenly I saw what I had been missing about Christ's second coming. The second coming doesn't just mean the end to certain things we've been doing. It means being with Jesus.

PHIL: Yes, that's right. He'll be here. That's better than any old baseball team.

KATHIE: Exactly. I guess that's why people in the church have always looked eagerly to his return. It's not just that Jesus would get them out of a tight spot or put an end to their aches and pains. The good thing will be that we'll be with the one we love.

BLANCHE: You're right, my dear.

KATHIE: I think even this Advent wreath should remind us of his coming. The light isn't very bright, but when we blow out the candles they remind us that perhaps soon the real light will come again and we'll have no more use for Advent wreaths. Don't you see?

HENRY *(hugging her)*: I see that I didn't raise a stupid, rattle-brained daughter like I thought I did a few minutes ago. I raised a pretty smart girl.

PHIL: Ugh! Can she read the prayer now and get this over with?

BLANCHE: Read it, Kathie.

KATHIE: All right. "Lord Jesus, we are waiting for you. Our lives need you. Our hearts yearn for you. Lord Jesus, come quickly and fill all the world with your light. We ask it in your name, Amen." *(All have been praying with her.)*

ALL: Amen.

HENRY: Now, Phil.

PHIL *(blows out the candles):* At last!

Jesus Is Best

Text: Luke 21:25-27

Human beings enjoy calamities. We don't like them to happen to us, of course, but when the house in the next block catches fire, we're there. If there is an accident on the highway, we want to stop even if it is obvious that there are already enough people present to help the injured. We all read newspapers and watch TV avidly when there is a disaster or threatened trouble in any corner of the world.

Perhaps it is this interest in calamities that explains why so many people are fascinated by ideas about the end of the world. The signs mentioned in our text are interpreted a dozen ways. Men try to read all the riddles of the Book of Revelation. A book like *The Late Great Planet Earth* quickly becomes a bestseller. We are all somewhat like the old lady in the play, *The Giant Staircase,* who enjoyed scaring herself.

This fascination with calamity isn't so bad in itself. A few goosebumps now and then don't harm any of

us. Perhaps it is better to be unduly concerned about
the end of our world than to be so involved in day
by day living that we give no thought to the future.
However, speculation about the events connected
with the second coming of Christ mislead us. Such
ideas cause us to think about the second coming
rather than the second coming of *Christ.* And the
accent should be on him. For Christianity is a one-
man religion. It centers in one person. We do not
have a faith founded on a book or on a statement of
doctrine, but our faith depends on a personal relationship between Christ and ourselves. Christianity
is Christ, and Christ is Christianity.

Jesus himself understood and proclaimed that
truth. His statements about his own person are either
true, or they comprise the worst bragging ever done
by man. To begin with, Jesus declared of the Old
Testament scriptures, "It is they that bear witness to
me." He insisted, "I am the way, the truth and the
life." He said, "I am the vine, you are the branches."
Jesus called men to follow *him,* not simply to follow
some kind of religious life. Even in our text, which
hints at some of the disasters which will occur at the
end of time, the stress is on the coming of the Son
of man with power and great glory. Jesus made no
effort to conceal the future glory which would be
his. We would call a man who proclaimed that he
would return to earth in a cloud a megalomaniac.
And so he would be if the statement weren't true.

Christianity rises and falls with Jesus. The enemies
of Christianity have always understood that. When
our Lord was here on this earth, the sharp attacks
were always personal. The Jewish and Roman leaders
arrested Jesus and seemed totally uninterested in the

disciples until after Pentecost. From that day to this, men have directed their criticism at Christ, denying his divinity or even his very existence. When attacks have been levelled at the church, the basis of the objections has been that Christianity hasn't been true to its founder. "The last Christian," someone has called Jesus.

Christians generally have also understood that they are called to a personal relationship with Jesus. Thumb through any church hymnal and notice how frequently the name of Jesus appears. Look at the church calendar and note that our celebrations are almost all centered in Christ: his birth, his epiphany, his suffering, his death, his resurrection. Paul recognized the nature of faith when he declared: "For I decided to know nothing among you except Jesus Christ and him crucified." Luther in his advice to preachers stated: "We preach always him, the true God and man. This may seem a limited and monotonous subject, likely to be soon exhausted, but we are never at the end of it."

How is it with you? Do you know him? Is he the one who is at the center of your faith, or do you simply believe in some vague religiosity? True Christians find that it is Jesus who gives meaning to life. He is the one who rejoices when we rejoice and also the one who helps us through the dark periods of life. Clarence Macartney, famous Presbyterian preacher, tells of the woman who came to him to tell of her troubles and problems. But she also was aware that she had been able to surmount all of her difficulties. As she talked, she said, almost to herself, "Oh, if I had not known him. . . . " The statement was incomplete but the great preacher realized where the woman had gotten the source of her strength. For Christianity is Jesus. He enables us to live the victorious life.

Yet there is something missing in this picture. A famous hymnwriter put his finger on the difficulty when he wrote:

> Jesus, the very thought of thee
> With sweetness fills the breast;
> But sweeter far thy face to see,
> And in thy presence rest.

There's the flaw. Jesus has been here, but he is not here today. You and I are caught between two Advents. In a way we are not much better than the people of the Old Testament. They waited for a Messiah to come. We wait for a Lord to return.

We find ways to bridge this separation: prayer, communion, symbols, etc. Yet while we should not disparage such helps, they are a poor substitute for the real thing. Think of prayer. It is a blessed thing to pray and we feel assured that our Lord hears our prayers, and yet what a joy it would be to have him give us a personal answer. We come to communion and we believe he is truly present in the sacrament, and yet what a poor substitute bread and wine are for the living person of our Lord. In the Advent wreath used in our play the candles are symbols of the one who is the light of the world, and yet what is a candle in comparison with Jesus himself.

Actually we are in the position of a lover who receives letters from his sweetheart or wife. It is certainly nice to receive the letters, but no true lover would say that he preferred the letters to the presence of his beloved. We are thankful for the Holy Spirit who gives us a promise of the future, but it isn't the same as achieving that future. That's why the second coming is important to us. There are many wonderful things promised in the Bible for the believer. We will have a new heaven and a new earth. We will be free from pain and sin and death. But all these things fade into nothingness compared with the fact that we will be with Jesus. That will be best of all.

And this is the truth that we need to cling to in the midst of the troubles of this world. We believe that just as truly as he was born in Bethlehem, he will return for his own. We may be confused about many of the prophecies and the events in connection with Christ's second coming. It may not be too clear just how the signs will occur that mark his return. The Christian may wonder about the millenium mentioned in the Book of Revelation. Bible scholars disagree as to whether we will all live on this earth or someplace else for eternity. Perhaps the Bible is purposely obscure at this point. But the details are unimportant so long as we know that *he* will return.

When a cease fire agreement in Vietnam was signed, American prisoners of war began to return. The papers were full of descriptions of how the men were released, where they were flown to, and what hospital care they received. I suppose some people were very interested in these details but I doubt that the people who were expecting sons and husbands and fathers from whom they have been separated cared much about the mechanics of the operation. They simply wanted to be reunited with their loved ones.

So it is with us. We have a promise for the future. We are like people who have read a book and know it will all come out right in the end. We know that the time will come when the separation between the Christian and the Lord will be at an end. That gives us courage for today and hope for tomorrow. We are going to be with Jesus. And that is best.

THIRD SUNDAY IN ADVENT
LUKE 1:26-38

DRAMA

The Book

MEDITATION

God Planned This

The Book

CHARACTERS

MARY: an old woman, rather feeble, but still able to summon fire at times

DEBORAH: companion of Mary, a bit soft and sentimental

RACHEL: companion of Mary, harder and sharper than Deborah

LUKE: author of the third Gospel, fairly young, mild-mannered

SETTING

A simple Palestinian home. Several benches are needed and there can be a draped table. But the scene should not reflect wealth but poverty. The characters wear simple Palestine costumes, long tunics or robes. The costumes should not be too fancy. LUKE carries a scroll and can have the passage typed on it. Use two heavy dowels and some parchment or brown paper for the scroll.

As the scene opens, DEBORAH *is helping* MARY *across stage to the bench off center.*

DEBORAH: Careful, careful, Mary. *(They reach bench.)* There. There you are. (MARY *sits.*)

MARY: Thank you, Deborah. I'm afraid I can't walk the way I used to.

DEBORAH: Oh no! You do very well for—for . . . *(Groping for word.)*

MARY: For an old woman, you were going to say.

DEBORAH *(shocked):* No, no.

MARY: Yes. And you're right. I get weaker every day. It's so good of you and Rachel to take care of me. But where is Rachel?

DEBORAH: She's in the kitchen, doing some last minute cleaning.

MARY: Does she think our visitor is going to inspect the kitchen? But I guess it can stand a cleaning.

DEBORAH: She never seems to get tired of scrubbing and dusting. But here she comes now. *(Looking off stage.)*

RACHEL *(enters and runs over to* MARY*):* Mary, are you in here already? Are you all right? Did Deborah help you? Why didn't you call me? I hope you didn't overdo yourself.

MARY: Rachel, you'll have to stop treating me like a fragile piece of Grecian pottery. I can take care of myself—with a little help.

RACHEL: Well, I'm not sure having a visitor today is going to help you much. What's he coming for anyway? He was here before and talked to you almost the whole morning. That should have been enough for him. (*Crosses stage so she and* DEBORAH *are on same side, where* LUKE *will enter.*)

MARY: Rachel, Dr. Luke is just being kind. I told him what he wanted to know when he was here the other time. Today he's coming back to read to me the things he has written so I can be sure the record is just the way it should be. After all, he *is* writing the story of my son, so it's important that there should be no mistakes in the book.

DEBORAH: I can hardly wait to hear what Dr. Luke has written.

RACHEL: I'm sure he thinks it's necessary for him to visit today. But everyone seems to have some *important* reason for bothering you. Every believer who comes to Jerusalem has to stop in and see you. (*Imitating*) "Must see the mother of our Lord, just for a moment," they plead. And you always agree to see them.

MARY: If it makes them happy, I'm willing to see a thousand visitors a day. It's little enough I can do. I can't preach or teach. I can't even sew for the poor any more.

RACHEL: You did enough. If it hadn't been for you, there wouldn't have been any Jesus or any church or any salvation for us.

DEBORAH: That's right.

MARY: Oh, you two! Do you think God couldn't have found a way to accomplish what he wanted done, even if one peasant woman had failed him?

RACHEL *(shocked):* You're not a peasant. You're of the house and lineage of David.

MARY *(gaily):* And you, my dear Rachel, are a bit of a snob. *(Knock on door.)* That sounds like our visitor. Deborah, let him in.

DEBORAH *(last minute straightening):* Yes, Mary. Oh, I hope everything looks all right.

RACHEL *(wiping off some dust):* I've certainly done my best.

MARY *(laughing as knock comes again):* You two fussy women! Let the poor man in.

DEBORAH *(opening door and greeting visitor):* Dr. Luke! Come in. We've been expecting you.

LUKE *(enters):* Thank you. It's Deborah, isn't it?

DEBORAH *(pleased):* Oh, yes sir. You remembered.

RACHEL: And I'm Rachel. Welcome. But don't tire her out.

MARY: Rachel!

LUKE: I'll be careful, Rachel. Good day, Mary, mother of our Lord. *(Bows.)*

MARY: You say it like it was one word. I suppose it is by now. Like most mothers I exist only in my son. Welcome, Dr. Luke.

LUKE: Don't get up. I'll sit right beside you. *(Sits on bench.)* Are you well, gracious lady?

MARY: I am well—for an old woman.

DEBORAH: Mary!

MARY: Deborah wants me to deny what my bones tell me is true. I *am* old. But soon, soon I will be young again. *(Looks at scroll.)* You have brought your book, I see.

LUKE: Yes. It is almost finished. And I suppose I'd better begin reading to you the parts I want you to hear before Rachel decides that my time is up.

MARY *(smiling):* She's as curious as the rest of us to hear what you have written. Take your time.

LUKE *(unrolls scroll):* The first part of the book deals with the story of Zacharias and Elizabeth. I'll skip that part and begin with the things you and I spoke about before.

DEBORAH: I can hardly wait.

LUKE: *(Reads Luke 1:26-38.)*

DEBORAH: Oh, how beautiful. *(Pause.)*

LUKE *(to* MARY*)*: Did I write it the way you wanted it said?

MARY *(who has been dreaming):* Yes, it's just right. Suddenly it all came back to me: that special night, the voice of the angel, the sense of another world close to ours, the bittersweetness of the message and all. I don't suppose I slept a moment that night after Gabriel left me. The air seemed filled with music, and yet I couldn't hear any sounds. The room was full of light, and yet it was dark. How strange to relive that moment again after all these years. *(Lapses into silence.)*

LUKE: Did you like the story, Rachel? *(Standing.)*

RACHEL: It's beautifully written and just the way Mary has told it to us many times. But Dr. Luke, you certainly don't propose to keep that story in your book, do you?

LUKE *(amazed):* Of course. I came today simply to check the details with Mary. The book is almost finished.

RACHEL: But you mustn't include *that* story. It would be a terrible mistake.

LUKE: I don't understand. You said yourself that I had written the story just the way Mary has told it to you. It *is* true.

RACHEL: I know it's the truth. I would not doubt Mary's word. Besides, many in the church have heard her say something about this before. But Dr. Luke, the whole story is going to give people the wrong impression.

LUKE: How can my writing do that?

RACHEL *(confidentially):* Look, you and I know Mary. She's loving and kind. She's aware of the great honor God conferred on her, but she's not proud. She even called herself a peasant woman just before you came. But you have no idea how pilgrims to Jerusalem already flock around her. There are some here in this house almost every day.

LUKE: I suppose people are naturally curious.

RACHEL: And also inclined to have romantic notions. Let them learn about Mary talking to angels and being overshadowed by the Holy Ghost, and they'll forget all about the simple Mary, mother of Jesus, that we all love.

LUKE: I hadn't thought of that.

RACHEL: Well, you'd better think about it. I tell you they'll make a superhuman being out of her. They'll squeeze out all her humanity, all the loveliness of her nature. Sometimes it seems they've already done that to her son, making him seem strange and inhuman. Now the same thing could happen to her. But it must not happen. You must remove this story from your book, or you'll spoil Mary's name for all times.

DEBORAH: Rachel, you've got it all wrong. You don't understand people!

RACHEL *(stung):* Why Deborah, you're the gushy, unrealistic one in this house! I tell you I know how people will react! *(The quarrel should get loud.)*

DEBORAH: Maybe sometimes, but not in this case. You think people have romantic minds. I believe they have evil minds. They'll not make Mary a superhuman being. They'll make her a sinful woman. They'll say she deceived Joseph, and they'll whisper that the father of Jesus wasn't God but some Roman soldier or some rascally publican and traitor.

LUKE: There have already been some whispers along that line, I must confess.

DEBORAH: Exactly. Once this story is written down, there'll be more than whispers. People will say you invented this miraculous birth to cover up a scandal.

RACHEL: Poof! Who cares about a few scandal mongers?

DEBORAH: I care! I don't want Mary's name dragged in the mud. And that's what people will do.

RACHEL: Deborah, the enemies of Jesus will find a thousand lies to attack him. That won't do the church any harm. It's the miracle-mongering friends who'll cause the trouble.

DEBORAH: You always insist that you know best. But this time I'm right!

RACHEL: I say you're not! You're—

LUKE: Ladies, ladies! It seems to me that you're both on the same side in this argument.

RACHEL: What do you mean? The same side indeed!

LUKE: Well, Rachel, you want me to leave the story out of the book. And now it sounds like Deborah also wants it omitted. Is that right?

DEBORAH: Yes. When you first read it, I was carried away. It's such a beautiful story. But then I realized that not everyone would hear it the way I did. People take the most beautiful things and twist them into something ugly and evil. I think you shouldn't give them that chance, Dr. Luke. You ought to remove this story from your book.

RACHEL: Now you're talking sense.

LUKE: Are you both agreed that the story should be removed?

DEBORAH *and* RACHEL: Yes, yes.

RACHEL: You must do it.

DEBORAH: Please reconsider.

LUKE: Well, you've made me think. I thought God's Spirit was guiding me to include the story, but maybe I misunderstood. If you're so sure. . . .

MARY *(has almost seemed asleep during the argument. She struggles to her feet):* Just a minute.

RACHEL *(rushes over to* MARY*)*: Mary, don't exert yourself.

DEBORAH: Here, let me help you.

MARY *(waving them back):* No. I have something to say and I think I have strength enough to say it. Alone. This is *my* story, and *I* want to be consulted.

LUKE: Yes, of course. We had forgotten you in the heat of our argument. Please guide us, good lady.

MARY: I intend to do that. What Deborah and Rachel say is true. Both of them are right. Some will exaggerate my part, and others will dirty my name.

DEBORAH: I'm glad you see it our way.

RACHEL: Yes. You must be guided by your friends.

MARY: I don't need you two to tell me what people will say about me. I learned that in my own household. I heard the reproach of unfaithfulness thrown at me by my own husband, Joseph. He had known me almost all my life, and yet he could imagine that I would deal falsely with him. And then when he found out the truth, he treated me as if I were an angel, rather than a simple woman of Galilee. I know how people's minds work. But Dr. Luke, I say the story should be told.

DEBORAH: But why, Mary, why?

RACHEL: It will just mislead people.

MARY: Some people, perhaps. But you don't see. You have all forgotten one person in the story—God. It's not my story or Dr. Luke's story. It's God's story. God told me, and through me the whole world, that man's salvation was God's doing. Jesus wasn't my idea. What happened wasn't the result of chance or of some human being's devising a way to save others. It was God, Yahweh, the God of Israel, planning and acting and uniting himself with mankind in my son. And it's important that all people know that.

LUKE: But you are involved, Mary. You had to consent. God didn't force you to be the mother of our Lord.

MARY: Of course God didn't make me accept his will. God never does. Isn't it wonderful that the one who holds the earth in the palm of his hand and guides the stars in his heaven was willing to ask the consent of a poor peasant woman—yes peasant woman, Rachel—before he put his plan to work? That's part of the meaning of the story. God acts with might and power, but he condescends to our weakness and humanity when he acts. There's only one explanation for that—love. And the love of God for mankind is a far greater miracle than anything that happened to me. I say, Dr. Luke, that the story of Jesus' birth ought to be told. What happens to my name isn't important.

DEBORAH: You make us ashamed of ourselves.

RACHEL: I can't oppose you. You see more than we do.

LUKE: The story will remain in the book.

MARY *(sits):* Good. Now go on with the next section.

LUKE: Gladly. *(He begins to read Luke 2. Voice fades out and the lights go down. If there is no other way to indicate the end of the scene, organ music of a familiar Advent hymn can be used, swelling in volume as* LUKE'S *voice fades out.)*

God Planned This

Text Luke 1:26-38

"Born of the Virgin Mary." Those five words in the creed have been the source of countless disputes in the church. The Virgin Birth of Jesus has become a kind of shibboleth in many circles, a distinguishing badge to determine whether a man is a theological conservative or a liberal. The arguments have been hot and heavy in religious circles for many years. Unfortunately no one is edified by argument; and when preachers quarrel, the average church member becomes disgusted, and rightly so.

Quite frankly, if the Virgin Birth of Jesus is simply a doctrine to argue about or a part of the creed to be repeated on Sunday, it is a useless teaching. Christianity is not an accumulation of doctrines—no matter how interesting such doctrines may seem to be. The material written in the Bible and confessed by the church is important because it conveys a message to the believer. Every teaching is intended to provide us with guidance and help. The Word of God is not history for the sake of history, nor poetry to please

our ears. There is no more utilitarian book in the
world than the Bible. John 20:31 is a pretty good
summary of the goal of all the Scriptures: "These are
written that you may believe that Jesus is the Christ,
the Son of God, and that believing you may have
life in his name."

But what on earth can be the message behind the
Virgin Birth? How can such an event speak to us in
the twentieth century? To understand this, we must
begin a long time before the days of Mary and Jesus.
The Virgin Birth must be seen as one link in a long
chain reaching back to the beginnings of God's deal-
ings with men. Anyone who studies the Bible becomes aware that both Old and New Testaments
stress that God is the source of our salvation. Although there are thousands of characters described
or at least mentioned in the Bible, careful analysis
shows that there is only one main actor—God himself. The Scriptures are well described as *The Book
of the Acts of God.*

Consider! God called Abraham from his home to
move to a new strange land. God promised Abraham
and later his descendants, Isaac and Jacob, that they
would eventually inherit that land. God called Moses
to deliver Israel from Egypt when the people were
in bondage. God led his people into Palestine when
the time had come for the fulfillment of his promise.
God put David on the throne of Israel and promised
that his family would possess that throne forever.
Despite the people's sin, God again delivered Israel
from captivity and restored them to their homeland
after they had been carried into exile by the Babylo-
nians. At every step in Israel's history, God is the
actor; he is the impetus behind every event.

Do you see what that says to us? It tells us that salvation comes from God, that it is his desire, his idea, his plan. But since he had the impetus every step of the way, does it seem logical that he would cease to act in the case of Jesus who was the culmination of his plan? Hardly! The Virgin Birth is not a strange doctrine dredged up from some pagan myth, as men have contended. It is not a poetic way of describing the act of conception. It simply represents the next move in a series of events that goes back to Abraham or even to Adam. God is always the one who acts. Every step on the way to man's salvation originates with God. He moves. He plans. He acts, and man reacts.

That is why the Annunciation to Mary belongs in the Advent season. For Advent is the time when we take a careful look at God's plans. It is the time when we see how the Old Testament prophets pointed to the coming Messiah, to the culmination of God's action for Israel and for the world. This doesn't mean that we look for specific predictions or exact correspondence between prophecy and fulfillment. Whether Isaiah literally prophecied the Virgin Birth or not isn't important. For in Advent we want to see the whole panorama of history, with everything moving toward one central point: the coming of Jesus Christ into the world. The Virgin Birth then must be seen as a part of the whole picture, not as a source of argument or as a test of orthodoxy. It is one more assurance to you and to me that God intended from the beginning to save men from their sins and that he did not neglect any step in that action.

Modern man however finds the Virgin Birth a scientific stumbling block. We say, "How can this be?" We find miracles hard to believe, and we suppose we are unique in that matter. People in Bible times must have been more credulous. But note that Mary asked the same question that we are tempted to ask, how can this be? Note further that according to Matthew's account it took a special dream from heaven to convince Joseph that Mary was with child by God's intervention. The other biblical miracles were often met with raised eyebrows by the people of Jesus' day. Even the disciples found it hard to grasp the fact of the Resurrection. The notion that people once were gullible but are now very scientific isn't borne out by the facts.

Actually, of course, you and I have evidence of actions by God that make the Virgin Birth seem a very minor miracle. In our day men have begun to glimpse the vastness of God's creation, and we are also beginning to understand some of the complex secrets of life. The God who could make a universe like ours, who could plan the intricate structure of the human eye, who could create a sunset or a songbird, would have no difficulty about a miracle like the Virgin Birth. William Blake, in his famous poem "Tiger," reveals the sense of awe that should overwhelm us when we look at God's world:

> When the stars threw down their spears
> And watered heaven with their tears,
> Did he smile his work to see?
> Did he who made the Lamb make thee?

When we look at the tiger and the lamb, we should not be balked by the idea of the Virgin Birth of Jesus.

Actually every saved Christian is a greater miracle than Christ's birth of the Virgin Mary. That God can change us from sinful creatures to new people in Christ—now that's a miracle that takes some believing. Yet God saved Saul the persecutor, redeemed Augustine the libertine, and changed John Newton, a slavetrader, into the author of "Amazing Grace." Perhaps the best answer to those who question the Virgin Birth is the reply of the angel to Mary, "With God nothing will be impossible."

We might stop here. That seems like a nice ending to the story. Luke might have followed the angel's account with his last line, "And the angel departed from her." The matter has been decided. God has made his plans. But God doesn't deal with his children that way. Before the matter was finally settled, Mary had to give her consent. Only then did the angel depart. For God doesn't force his will upon any human being. Sometimes we wish he would make people behave or at least restrain evil men from their actions. But God made us in his image. He does not degrade us by treating us like part of the furniture in his universe.

This waiting for consent is also a part of the pattern in the Bible. It is always a pattern of offer and response. Thus God told Abraham to leave his home, but Abraham had to go. God had David anointed as future king, but David had to choose to follow God— and at times he didn't do very well. God gave his people the chance to return from exile, but many preferred the comforts of their new homeland to the rigors of rebuilding Jerusalem. The choice always had to be made by man.

You and I get similar consideration from God. He

will not make you come to church. He will not make you read the Bible or believe in him. The Holy Spirit "calls, gathers, and enlightens" but he does not force. It is an amazing example of the patience of the Almighty that he allows us to refuse and reject his grace.

Thus the Virgin Birth mirrors the whole relationship between God and man. New life, new birth, is available to all. It is marvelous, wonderful, unbelievable. But in every instance we have the power of rejection. The picture of Christ standing at the door and knocking is the proper picture of the Christian life. The reply of Mary, "Behold I am the handmaid of the Lord," is the proper Christian response.

FOURTH SUNDAY IN ADVENT
I John 4:10-11

DRAMA

The Baby

MEDITATION

Is It Practical?

The Baby

CHARACTERS

> EDITH ROGERS: middle-aged, gentle churchwoman
>
> BOB ROGERS: middle-aged, a bit domineering but not too hard
>
> JIM ROGERS: older teen-ager, slightly rebellious but not alienated

SETTING

> A simple living room. Three chairs and a small table are all that are needed but other furniture can be added as desired.

As the scene opens, BOB *is reading the paper.* EDITH *is seated at the table with envelopes piled in front of her. She signs the last one, puts a stamp on the envelope.*

EDITH (*sighing*): Well, that's the last one. All the Christmas cards are addressed and stamped. I'm always glad when that chore is finished.

BOB: So am I.

EDITH: It doesn't seem to concern you. You never bother with anything that has to do with Christmas.

BOB: No, you can mark me down as another Scrooge. But you always do a good job, Edith, with the cards and presents and the Christmas dinner and everything.

EDITH: I try, anyway.

BOB: Who'll be here for dinner this year? The usual crowd of relatives?

EDITH: The usual crowd.

BOB: Oh well, it's just once a year.

EDITH: Yes, dear. And now I want to ask you a favor.

BOB: I know what it is. And the answer is the same as last year. I will *not* go to Christmas services with you and Jim. That's final.

EDITH: But why, Bob? It's only for an hour, once a year. It would make me so proud to have all three of us together there on Christmas.

BOB: Edith, I'll go to church with you any Sunday that you ask me. But not on Christmas.

EDITH: You're even beginning to sound like Scrooge.

BOB: I can't help that. I refuse to listen to the kind

of drivel people are forced to hear at Christmastime in church.

EDITH: Bob, that's not nice.

BOB: I can't help that. It's the truth. Look, Edith. The world today is filled with hatred and violence. The newspapers print nothing but ugly stories about war and robberies and murder. The evening TV news always sounds like *This Is Your FBI*. And then you expect me to go to church and hear a preacher drool about a little child who's supposed to bring peace and understanding to this earth. If ever anyone sent a boy to do a man's work, that was it.

EDITH: But Jesus grew up, Bob. The minister doesn't mean that a baby saved the earth.

BOB: I know he grew up. But that didn't make any difference. Such a Savior. Telling us to love our enemies, advising us to turn the other cheek, preaching peace and brotherhood to people who don't even understand the meaning of the words. It's disgusting. It didn't do Jesus much good to be peaceful and loving. The cross in your church tells you where he ended up.

EDITH: But Bob . . . .

BOB: Edith, what this world needs is somebody with power to deal with the crooks and murderers and dictators and communists and everyone who threatens good decent people. And all the church talks about is love. *(Sarcastic.)* "Love God. Love your neighbor." Love won't do it. Love can't do it. All the people who go around singing, *(mockingly)*

"What the world needs now is love, sweet love," ought to have their heads examined. Or confiscated, maybe.

EDITH: But Bob . . . .

BOB: I don't want to talk about it anymore. I'm not going to church this Christmas or next Christmas or any other Christmas, so let's not discuss it again. *(Softening.)* I don't mean to be cross, dear, but we just don't agree on that subject, so we'll have to agree to disagree.

EDITH: All right, dear. But there's something else I want to discuss with you. It's Jim.

BOB: What kind of trouble is he into now?

EDITH: He's not into any trouble. But the fact you asked such a question just emphasizes what's bothering me.

BOB: What do you mean by that?

EDITH: It's just that you and Jim seem to be always at odds lately. You're always arguing and fighting about things. You don't like the way he dresses, and you criticize his friends and laugh at his ideas. I don't like to see father and son going on like that.

BOB: Edith, to use his expression, the boy bugs me.

EDITH: I know. At times he's not easy to understand. And I'm not saying it's all your fault when you two fight. But growing up isn't so simple these days.

BOB: If he'd just grow up, I wouldn't complain.

EDITH: Well, he's doing better about things. But we both need to be a little more understanding.

BOB: I wish I could understand what he does with all the money that I give him.

EDITH *(stroking his face):* Dear, promise me that you'll be a little kinder to him this Christmas. That would be the nicest present you could give me.

BOB: Oh, all right. But it won't be easy. If I talked to my dad the way Jim talks to me sometimes . . . .

EDITH: But you didn't, dear. You probably thought the same things but you didn't have the nerve to say them.

BOB: Edith!

EDITH *(noise off stage):* Shh! Here he comes. Now try to be nice to him.

JIM *(hustles into the room):* Hello Mom, Dad. I'm glad to find you both here at the same time. I've got something to say.

BOB: How much is it going to cost me this time?

EDITH: Bob!

JIM: You don't need to worry, Dad. This time it's going to save you money. I've got a special announcement to make.

BOB: Sound the trumpets!

JIM: That's a good idea. You see, I've got a job.

EDITH: After school, dear? That's nice.

JIM: No, not after school. Full-time at Jones' garage.

That's the first part of the announcement. And the second part is—I'm quitting school.

EDITH: Oh no, you mustn't.

BOB: I forbid it.

JIM: But you can't forbid it. I'm of age, and I'm not only quitting school, but I'm moving out of the house. Bill Thompson has an apartment, and he wants someone to share it with him. We can live there real cheap. We can do our own cooking, and come and go as we please, and not be a burden to anybody.

EDITH: But Jim. We'll miss you so much. And at Christmastime too.

JIM: I'm sorry about it being right now. But the job and the apartment just opened up. I've got to grab both of them while I have the chance.

BOB: Now wait a minute! Nobody's quitting school and nobody's moving out of the house. Jim, you didn't even have the courtesy to talk this over with us before you made up your mind. Now sit down and let's talk about this move.

JIM *(gets loud):* Talk about it? That would only mean doing what *you* wanted me to do. That's the way it's always been when we talked about anything. For once in my life I want to make up my own mind! That's why I decided first and then told you.

EDITH: Now, now. Let's not get excited.

JIM: I'm not excited. I'm simply standing up for my

rights. I'm of age, and I'm going to do what I want to do.

BOB: You're just bluffing. You're my son, and I say you're staying here and you're going to finish school.

EDITH: I wish you would stay, Jim, what with Christmas coming and everything.

BOB: It's not a question of Christmas.

JIM: No, it's a question of getting away from here, of being someplace where people aren't yelling at me all the time. It's a question of feeling important and of not being someone who's supposed to do what he's told and not ask any questions.

BOB: That'll be the day. You've fought and argued over every decision I've made for the past five years.

JIM: Yes, because you've always been the one who made them. Well, I'm getting out. I've had enough.

BOB: You'll not leave home. You've got things too nice and cozy here. You've been talking like this for the past year or so.

JIM: I'll show you this is no threat. I'm going upstairs now and pack.

EDITH: Bob, you can't let him leave like this. Not with both of you so angry.

BOB: Jim, sit down!

JIM: Out of my way! I'm leaving. Bill Thompson has

a truck and he'll be here in an hour to help me haul my things to the apartment. *(Pushes* Bob *aside.)*

EDITH: Jim, you pushed your father!

JIM: I'm sorry. But you two don't seem to realize that I mean business.

BOB *(slowly):* I'm beginning to realize it. But look, Jim. Is it asking too much to want you to sit down and talk for a minute? That truck will wait for you.

JIM *(suspicious):* Why should I sit down and talk?

BOB: Maybe we can still iron things out. I didn't mean to pull rank and yell at you. I just thought you were being dramatic and self-important.

JIM: Well, I wasn't. I'm simply fed up.

BOB: But we don't want you to leave. Imagine what the relatives will think when they come for Christmas dinner.

JIM: So that's what's worrying you. What people will think. Well, I don't care. I'm going.

BOB: Please don't.

JIM: I'm moving. Unless—unless you can give me one good reason why I should stay.

BOB: Well, I—I—.

JIM: You see, you've run out of threats. And you don't even know one real reason why I should continue to live here.

BOB *(Pause. Then, as though beaten):* Yes, there is a

reason. But I don't suppose it will make any difference.

JIM: What is it? What is it?

BOB: It's very simple. You're my son, and I love you, Jim.

JIM: *You what?*

BOB: You heard me. I said I love you and I mean it. I know I haven't said that very often.

JIM: You *never* said that to me.

BOB: Maybe you're right. I guess it's a hard thing for me to say. But I do love you the way a father loves his son. I suppose that's why I've yelled at you and fussed at you and grumbled and complained all these years. It's a strange way to show love, I know. But there it is.

JIM: I never would have guessed it. For years you've found fault with everything I've said or done. You've criticized me before my friends and tried to keep me from doing what I've wanted to do.

BOB: I know, I know. But Jim, I only meant it for your own good.

JIM: I suppose you did. But you never said you loved me. I didn't know.

BOB: Well, you know it now. Only I'm not offering that as a reason for you to stay. I suppose it's too late for you to change your mind now. Too much has happened. I suddenly realize I've not been a very good father for you all these years. But I want you to go, knowing that I've loved you, despite all the shouting and the arguments.

EDITH: And I love you too, Jim.

JIM: I know that, mother. Well, you two really cut me down. It's too bad that a fellow has to leave home to find out things.

EDITH: I guess that's the way it is. We'll both come upstairs and help you pack now. I'm so glad that you and your father are friends again. And you'll be sure to come for Christmas dinner. Maybe you'll be willing to go to church with me on Christmas the way we've always done.

JIM: I will, Mom, I will. You know, somehow that job and that apartment don't seem so important now as they once did.

EDITH: Jim.

BOB: Jim, you mean . . . .

JIM: Look, I'm suddenly realizing some things too. I guess I haven't always made life easy for you two. Maybe I've given you cause to yell at me at times. And I'll probably do it again. But knowing that you love me makes a difference. If you want me to stay . . . .

EDITH: You know we do.

BOB: We can be a real family. Let's all try again.

JIM: Well, I'm willing. But I'll have to go and call Bill Thompson and tell him I'll not be needing that apartment. He'll have to find another guy.

Bob: O.K., son. You go make that call. (Jim *exits.*)

Edith: Thank God for that.

Bob: Yes, thank God I didn't speak too late. I guess a man gets so involved with little things in a family that he forgets the important thing—love.

Edith: I'm so happy, Bob. This is going to be a real Christmas.

Bob: That's right. All this started when we were talking about Christmas. Well, now I'll make you even a little happier. If you want me to, I'll go with you to that Christmas service this year.

Edith: That would be wonderful. But Bob, I know how you feel about Christmas. I don't want you to go if you don't want to.

Bob: It so happens that I *do* want to go. Don't think I'm getting soft in the head. But the past few minutes have made me do some thinking. If love can change Jim and me like that, maybe that baby born in Bethlehem will turn out to be right after all. Maybe love *can* change the world if we only give it a chance.

(The End. If desired, the first two lines of "Love Came Down at Christmas" can be sung offstage.)

Is It Practical?

Text: I John 4:10-11

One of the most powerful words in the English language today is *practical*. No matter what dreams you dream, no matter what proposals you make or what plans you devise, someone is sure to ask: "But is it practical?" And unless you can give a detailed and satisfactory answer to that question, nothing else will make any difference. Whatever is not practical is of no value to the hard-headed businessmen of today's world.

No one should quarrel with the requirement that all proposals must be practical. The world has suffered at times from the dreamers of impossible dreams. However I believe a Christian has cause to quarrel with the standards of measurement often used to determine what is practical. Take a look at some of the accomplishments of men when evaluated on the basis of practicality. Note the system we have evolved for settling the quarrels between nations. When nations cannot agree, they resort to war. They seek to destroy each other's land. They slaughter the strongest and finest of their manpower. And when one nation has been beaten or when both are totally exhausted, men conclude peace. That really isn't a very practical solution to the problem of disagreement, is it?

Or think how we deal with poverty and hunger in the world. God has so blessed this earth that there is sufficient for all of its inhabitants if the division of goods were fair. But the practical men of the world have so arranged things that some have too much while others live in poverty. As someone has said, "Half the world is starving and the other half is dieting." The enormous concentration of goods in the hands of a few seems neither fair nor wise. But this is the work of practical men.

Perhaps a third example will suffice. One of the most disturbing problems of our society is that of crime and violence. Men have reacted to the threat against property and life by seeking to apprehend the guilty and put them in jail for a period of their life. The theory is that such punishment will cure men of their tendency toward evil actions. The number of repeaters and the rising tide of crime in the world casts doubts upon the methods of practical men in dealing with evil.

What's wrong? Are human beings stupid by nature and thus unable to solve their problems? Hardly. But consistently men have forgotten one factor of human existence—the presence of God in life. Men have been atheists as far as their daily existence is concerned. They have overlooked one of the great messages of the Advent season: this is God's world and he is actively concerned in its welfare. There can be

no other explanation for the coming of Christ into
this earthly existence. God said by that action:
"Count me in, men. I am still in charge here."

Moreover God indicated how he would solve the
problem of men. He certainly didn't use his power
when he sent a baby to overcome man's sinfulness.
He didn't use threats or violence to make men behave. The whole story of Christ's coming is summed
up in that one four letter word—love. In the words
of Christian Rossetti:

> Love came down at Christmas,
> Love all lovely, love divine;
> Love was born at Christmas,
> Star and angels gave the sign.

This is God's solution to the problems of life. The
message of Advent is a message of love, of over-
coming evil with good. "He loved us and sent his
Son to be the expiation for our sins," John declares,
and in that simple phrase sums up God's practical
answer to men's needs.

Of course such a phrase evokes cynical remarks
from the practical men of the world. "It won't work,"
they say. Love is for romantic fools and starry-eyed
dreamers. Love isn't practical. You can't deal with
conflicts between nations by talking about love. You
can't solve the maldistribution of wealth by talking
about love. Above all, talking to a criminal about
love is like trying to rub custard into a block of
granite.

Maybe so. But the practical men of the world
haven't had much success with their techniques. We
have tried the way of hate and greed and punishment for centuries, and nothing has resulted but

more hate and greed and punishment. We have followed the advice of practical men, and the advice has simply compounded our problems. Isn't it time to take seriously God's program for man? To live in God's world and yet to ignore God's guidance seems the heart of folly. Advent is, therefore, not only a call to repentance but also a call to reality, to the recognition that God is a god of love who seeks to rescue his children from their own foolishness.

But before we all go marching out of the church singing, "What the world needs now is love, sweet love," please note the second half of our text. "Beloved, if God so loved us, we also ought to love one another." Do you catch that note? We ought to love one another. It doesn't do any good to recognize God's loving nature unless that thought provokes a response to love in our hearts. Remember Jesus' parable of the debtor who was forgiven a great debt by the king, but went out and seized a fellow man because he owed the great debtor a trifling sum. Nothing good came out of that action.

And nothing good comes from our Christian faith in a God of love unless *we* are moved to action. The man in our play could have known all about God's love, but that knowledge meant nothing until he said to his own son, "I love you." And in a similar way, Advent is a wonderful season for learning about God's great concern for man, but that knowledge will be useless unless we are moved to share that love with others.

Unfortunately here is where Christians so often fail. Think of how, even from our pulpits, we have preached hatred against our fellow men in time of war. Think of how Christian people have been as greedy for this world's goods as have their pagan neighbors, even salving their consciences at times by insisting that the poor are only getting what they deserved. And Christian people have not distinguished themselves in the showing of love toward the unfortunates in our society, but have often been the leaders in advocating harsh punishment and revenge.

The truth of the matter is that we must bear much of the guilt for what has happened in the world. The practical men have usually done what they thought best for society. But we have known better. We have had the light, indeed we are the light of the world and the salt of the earth. It is time that we accept our responsibility and call all people to live together in peace and love on this earth.

I am under no illusion that a few Christians practicing love will transform the world overnight and establish a utopia here on this earth. Bringing love to bear on the problems of life is a hard and difficult task and one that can be very frustrating. The Russian novelist Dostoevsky in *The Brothers Karamazov* says this very well when he pictures the Elder as saying:

> For love in action is a harsh and dreadful thing, compared to love in dreams. Love in dreams thirsts for immediate action, rapidly performed and in the sight of all. Men will even give their lives if only the ordeal does not last long but is soon over, with all looking on and applauding as though on the stage. But active love is labor and fortitude, and for some people, too, perhaps a whole science. But I predict that just when you see with horror that in spite of all your efforts you are getting farther from

your goal instead of nearer to it—at that very moment I predict that you will reach it and behold clearly the miraculous power of the Lord who has been all the time loving and mysteriously guiding you.

Those are wonderful words of encouragement for Christians to persist in their efforts to bring love to bear on the problems of this life.

There is a simple prayer that seems to sum up what has been said. It goes like this: "Lord, change the world, beginning with me." Beginning with me. May that be your advent prayer today and in all the days ahead. Amen.

DRAMA

The Ornament

MEDITATION

The Right Time

The Ornament

A living room where the family is trimming a small Christmas tree. The trimming is almost done. On stage left GRANDFATHER is asleep in an easy chair. There are some other chairs and the usual mess of paper and boxes that contained the decorations.

CHARACTERS

HAROLD: an older teenager

JILL: a few years younger than Harold but mature for her age

BOB: the youngest in the family, full of life

MOTHER: fairly young looking, pleasant, the peacemaker

GRANDFATHER: elderly, a bit cranky but not so unpleasant that we hate him

HAROLD (*fastens an ornament on the tree, then steps back to admire his work*): There. How do you think that looks? The tree is just about done, I'd say.

BOB: Done? Already? We just got started.

JILL (*looking critically at tree*): No, it's not done yet. It needs another ornament here. (*Indicates bare space in center.*)

MOTHER: That's right, Jill. A small golden ball will look nice there and we can use a few more icycles over on the right side.

BOB: O.K. O.K., I'll put them on. (*Starts to hang icycles by throwing them.*)

JILL: Don't just toss them. Hang them on. (*Puts golden ball in space.*) How's that? Did I get it in the right place?

MOTHER: Just right, Jill. Don't touch it.

BOB: How do the icycles look? Did I put enough on? Huh? Huh?

MOTHER: You did it just the way I wanted it done. The tree is finished. Don't add another thing.

HAROLD: It *is* a beautiful tree.

JILL: The best trimming job we've ever done.

BOB: Oh, you always say that.

JILL: Well, we ought to get better every year. Just like you ought to get smarter, only you don't.

BOB: Say . . . .

MOTHER: Now, you two. You've behaved better than usual today. Don't start anything now and spoil it. And the tree *does* look lovely.

HAROLD: Let's plug in the lights so we can see it all lit up.

BOB *(rushing for the wire):* I'll do it.

MOTHER: Careful, Bob or you'll knock the tree over.

BOB: There. *(Tree lights go on.)*

ALL: Oh!

JILL: It *is* beautiful. Makes me feel all trembly.

BOB *(disgusted):* Girls! *(To Mother.)* Now are you going to read the Christmas story to us, Mother? Like you always do?

MOTHER: Yes, I think we're about ready for that.

HAROLD: You think we ought to wake up grandpa? He fell asleep when I first started to put the lights on the tree. Slept through the whole trimming bit.

BOB: Wake him up. He ought to see the tree and hear the story too. Here, I'll wake him. *(Ready to shout.)*

JILL *(Puts hand over BOB's mouth):* Not so fast. He'll have plenty of time to see the tree later, and he knows the story. If you wake him now, he might think of *it.*

BOB: Huh?

HAROLD *(catching on):* That's right. Better let him sleep. You know grandpa has a thing about Christmas trees. His special ornament?

BOB: Oh yeah. Now I remember. We had an argument about it last year.

MOTHER: Well, we aren't going to have an argument this time. But I think we'd better let grandpa sleep for now.

GRANDFATHER (*yawning and stretching*): Hey. Somebody talking about me?

BOB: Oh boy. Now it starts.

GRANDFATHER: I must have fallen asleep. Looks like you've got the tree all trimmed.

HAROLD: Don't know how we did it without you, but there it is.

JILL: Every ornament is in the right place. The tree couldn't even stand another icycle.

MOTHER: The children did a beautiful job, didn't they, papa?

GRANDFATHER: Very good, very good. Only of course you'll have to make space for my special ornament.

JILL: Oh no!

HAROLD: Here we go again.

MOTHER: Children! (*Shakes her head.*)

GRANDFATHER: Surely you haven't forgotten about my special ornament?

MOTHER: No, we didn't forget it. But we thought maybe we wouldn't use it this year. The tree's small and the ornament might not look well with the other decorations.

GRANDFATHER: Nonsense. Just remove that golden ball in the front and hang my ornament there. You know my family brought it with them when they came from Germany. It's hung on trees in the Schmidt family home for 75 years.

BOB: Time to give it a rest.

GRANDFATHER: Don't be smart, young man!

JILL: Grandpa, can't we leave it off just this one time? It spoils the whole tree if you put that old ornament on it.

GRANDFATHER: Spoils it! No! it *makes* our tree. Nobody else in this town has an ornament like that. Now all of you stay right where you are and I'll go get it. I never let that old ornament get packed in with the other Christmas things for fear it might get lost or broken. But I know right where it is. *(Exits.)*

HAROLD *(bitterly)*: I'm sure he knows right where it is.

JILL: Mother, don't let him spoil our tree again.

HAROLD: That ornament is old and ugly.

BOB: It's icky.

MOTHER: I know, I know. But he has his heart set on it.

JILL: Well, I've got my heart set on *not* having that ornament on the tree this year. I'm going to tell him he can't hang it there this time. When my friends come over at Christmas, grandpa always has to point out his ornament and tell them all about it and the whole family history of the

Schmidt family and why they left Germany and
everything. It's so embarrassing.

HAROLD: Come to think about it, I think I could tell
the whole story myself. I've heard it so many
times.

BOB: Say, when he comes back, maybe I could bump
against him and break the old ornament. I'm
pretty clumsy, you know. At least, everybody says
I am.

MOTHER: Don't you dare do that, Bob. Let's all behave ourselves. Remember it's Christmas.

JILL: Well, why can't grandpa remember it's Christmas.

MOTHER: He's an old man.

HAROLD: Wasn't he ever young? Doesn't he remember how old people made nuisances of themselves
when he was young by having their own way about
everything?

MOTHER: I'm afraid we never remember.

BOB: I will when I get old.

HAROLD: If you don't stop getting into fights at
school, they may not even *let* you get old.

BOB: Awright.

JILL: But mother, I think we've got to take a stand
someplace, and it might as well be here. Grandpa
acts like a tyrant around here. He always has to
have his own way about everything. Won't even
discuss anybody else's views. Somebody has to
oppose him. And I'm going to do it today.

HAROLD: I'm on your side.

BOB: Me too. I like a good fight.

MOTHER *(distressed)*: Now children, children. Sh, I hear him coming.

GRANDFATHER *(enters, carrying the ornament in his hand. It is a large, old-fashioned ornament)*: There it is. I knew right where it was. Isn't it a beauty?

JILL: I think it's horrible looking. It'll spoil our tree, Grandpa. We're not going to have it hung there this year.

HAROLD: No we're not. We've made up our minds.

GRANDFATHER: What? What are you children saying?

HAROLD: We're saying you're not going to spoil our decorations this year by hanging that old thing on the tree. We're defying you, grandpa.

JILL: That's right. No old ornament and no long stories about the Schmidt family this year.

GRANDFATHER: Martha, do you hear what your children are saying?

MOTHER: I hear them, father. I didn't want them to argue with you like this. But they don't want the ornament on the tree this year. Couldn't we make an exception just this once?

GRANDFATHER: That's out of the question. If I want the ornament to go on the tree, that's where it goes. When I was young, children knew how to obey their elders. That's what's wrong with this world today. No respect for age.

HAROLD: We do respect you, grandpa. But does that have to include loving that old moth-eaten ornament?

GRANDFATHER: Moth-eaten! I'll have you know this was an expensive ornament when it was bought in Germany 75 years ago. It's better made than any of your modern junk. Years ago they knew how to make things to last.

JILL: They did—worse luck.

GRANDFATHER: Look here, can't you see what this ornament means to me? When I was young, it always hung on the Christmas tree in our house. The tree was lit with hundreds of candles, and they made the ornaments sparkle as no electric lights ever will do. After Christmas dinner we would sit around the table, and father would read the Christmas story to us from the family Bible. Then he would point out the ornament and tell us how the family left Germany and came to America and settled on the old family farm. There are a hundred memories in this old ornament.

JILL: But grandpa, Christmas is now, not then. We want to enjoy *our* Christmas, and you spoil it with that old ornament and with your long stories about Christmas a million years ago. Can't you see that?

GRANDFATHER: I only see that you don't have any respect for the past. But the ornament goes on the tree. Right here in place of that gold ball. *(Takes off the golden ball and hangs up the ornament.*

There. The ornament is in place. And anyone who touches it will be—will be—

HAROLD: Will be what?

GRANDFATHER: Will be cut out of my will. I mean it. *(Exits, angrily.)*

JILL *(starting to cry):* Oh mother, now he's spoiled everything. The tree and Christmas and all the rest.

HAROLD: The old grouch. For two cents I'd call his bluff and take the ornament off anyway, will or no will.

MOTHER: Now children, I warned you . . . .

JILL: It's not fair. Not fair.

BOB: I'm going to do something real mean to him. Just as soon as I think of something.

HAROLD: I'm not going down to the store for him anymore. He can go himself when he wants his cigars or magazines.

JILL: That's the idea. You've got to fight fire with fire. We'll make him sorry he was so mean to us.

MOTHER: Have you forgotten that it's Christmas, the time for love and good cheer?

JILL: Grandpa didn't show much love and good cheer. He was just mean.

MOTHER: And you think you'll get even by being mean in return?

HAROLD: What else can we do? But it does take all

the fun out of Christmas. I don't even feel like I want you to read the Christmas story to us now.

BOB: Me, neither.

JILL: What a day!

MOTHER: I have an idea. Suppose I read you a different version of the Christmas story this year. Just a short one?

HAROLD: Well, if you must. Should we clean up the papers and mess first?

MOTHER: No, this won't take long. But maybe it'll make you feel better about everything. Bob, hand me that Bible over there. Let me see. *(Leafing through.)* Oh, here it is. It's Galatians 4:4. It's about the fullness of time.

HAROLD: Oh, I know that.

JILL: So do I.

BOB: Well, I don't. Read it, mother. *(Children sit on the floor.)*

MOTHER: All right. *(Reading)* "But when the fullness of time was come, God sent his son as a great and terrible warrior to punish the people on this earth because they had been mean to God and he was determined to be mean to them in return."

HAROLD. Mother, that's not the way it goes.

JILL: God didn't send Jesus as a warrior. Jesus came as a baby in Bethlehem.

BOB: I don't think God hates us. He loves us. At

least that's what the teacher said in Sunday school last week.

MOTHER: Well, you don't seem to like that version of the Christmas story. Neither do I because it's not true. Even though men were mean and stubborn and rebellious, God didn't try to get even with them. He showed all of us love. That's the way God acts.

BOB: I get it. You're saying that's the way we ought to treat grandpa.

MOTHER: Am I?

HAROLD: Yes, you are. And you're right. I guess we should love him, even when he makes us angry.

BOB: You think we should go and apologize to him. Gee, I don't like to do that.

JILL: I suppose we should. Still . . . .

MOTHER: I think I know a better way. You know how much he loves some of those old German songs. Remember, he taught all of us to sing "O Tannenbaum" in German? Suppose we all sing that for him. Maybe that will say that we still love him.

BOB: Do you think it'll do any good? He was awful mad.

MOTHER *(smiling):* It's worth a try.

HAROLD: You start us off, Mother. I think we'll remember the words as we go along.

MOTHER: All right. *(They sing at least two verses of*

the song. Words are printed below. Another German hymn can be substituted if desired. If congregation is of another ethnic background, a Danish, Norwegian, English, etc. song can be substituted and appropriate changes can be made in the dialog.)

O Tannenbaum, O Tannenbaum,
Wie treu sind deine Blätter!
Du grünst nicht nur zur Sommerzeit,
Nein, auch im Winter, wenn es schneit.
O Tannenbaum, O Tannenbaum,
Wie treu sind deine Blätter!

O Tannenbaum, O Tannenbaum,
Du kannst mir sehr gefallen!
Wie oft hat nicht zur Weihnachtszeit
Ein Baum von dir mich hoch erfreut!
O Tannenbaum, O Tannenbaum,
Du kannst mir sehr gefallen!

GRANDFATHER *(appearing in doorway)*: That's my favorite Christmas song. I sang that at the church Christmas program when I was just a little boy.

JILL: We know you like that song, Grandpa. It's our way of saying that we love you. We're sorry we kicked up such a fuss.

HAROLD: We didn't stop to think what the ornament meant to you.

BOB: I almost broke it. On purpose. *(Hugs grandpa.)*

GRANDFATHER: Broke it. That's a good idea. I've been an old fool. Having my grandchildren love me is more important than any Christmas tree ornament. I'll break it myself. *(Grabs for the ornament.)*

MOTHER *(reaching for it):* No, no, father. Give it to me.

GRANDFATHER: But it's caused so much trouble.

MOTHER: We caused the trouble because we all wanted our own way. Christmas ought to be a time for being loving and respecting one another's feelings.

GRANDFATHER: But what are you going to do with the ornament?

MOTHER: It's very simple. I'm going to put it in the center of the table as a Christmas decoration. And since it's 75 years old, I'm going to call in Bob Jones and let you tell him all about those Christmases when you had this ornament on the family tree. He's a reporter for the newspaper, and I'm sure they'll print the story. Then everyone will know about your ornament, and you won't have to tell people about it any more.

BOB: Attaboy, mother!

GRANDFATHER: I always said I raised a smart girl there.

JILL: Mother, you're the greatest.

GRANDFATHER: Now, what do you say to singing the first verse of "O Tannenbaum" again and letting me join in? It'll sound good for the whole family to sing together.

BOB: Sure, grandpa. You and I can sing bass.

(ALL sing the song as they exit.)

The Right Time

Text: Galatians 4:4-5

It was the right time, "the fullness of time" as the King James translation puts it. God in his wisdom chose the right time to send his Son into the world. Men have been tempted to doubt God's choice in history. The prophets were ready for the Messiah long before he came. And in our day some have felt that the present would have been better than 4 B.C. for a Savior to appear. Judas in that rock opera *Jesus Christ Super-Star* sings at the end of the production:

Why'd you choose such a backward time
And such a strange land?
If you'd come today you would have reached a
    whole nation.
Israel in 4 B.C. had no mass communication.

But God who could see the whole stream of human history knew best when to enter it.

Certainly the physical conditions were favorable. When Jesus Christ was born, the world was at peace.

Men had a common government and understood a common language. There were roads that made travel throughout the empire easier than it had been for centuries. Looking back on the events we can see that many things were favorable for the spread of the gospel.

In addition, religious conditions were favorable. The old pagan religions had lost their hold on people. Men were seeking a new faith, a better understanding of God. Many had become converts to the Jewish faith because it offered a nobler picture of God and a higher standard of morality. But those who made the change found the legal codes of the Jewish religion a terrible weight. Indeed the Jews were having the same experience. Peter expressed the feelings of many when he declared at the first church council that the law was "a yoke which neither our fathers nor we have been able to bear." The world was ripe for the gospel. Perhaps there were other factors which made God choose the time which he did. We do not know. But it was the right time.

Yet all that is ancient history. And it is possible to get too involved in ancient history at Christmas time. The story is an appealing one. And men have exerted their best efforts in poetry, prose, art, and music to embellish the Christmas story. Moreover all of us tend to do what the grandfather did in our play—identify and surround the Christmas season with family memories and customs. All these things are not wrong in themselves. But they can become a menace if we identify the right time with something that happened in the past.

The real question is, is this the fullness of time

for us? Is this the right time for us? Christmas calls upon us to make this a season of renewal for our lives. Shepherds at the manger mean nothing unless we too worship the newborn king. Wise men are simply figures in history unless we also offer our gifts to this newborn king. And pleasant family memories remain just that unless the spirit of love permeates our hearts too. It was the right time. Is it still the right time for us?

It was the right way. We would never have thought of saving men by the method that God chose. "Born of a woman, born under the law," Paul says, and this strikes us as very strange. We still marvel at the baby in a manger. We would have chosen a king's palace or at least the home of some substantial citizen. We like the story of angels and of wise men and a star. That seems more in keeping with God and his dignity. Shepherds seem to throw a false note into the story

And yet it was the right way. Nobody can fault it now for this babe in a manger has become the Savior of mankind. Millions of people now confess that Jesus Christ has made a difference in their lives. The proof of the pudding in in the eating, we say, and Christmas has proven remarkably successful. The first verse from the Harvard Prize Hymn by Harry Webb Farrington puts the whole thing very well:

> I know not how that Bethlehem Babe
> Could in the God-head be;
> I only know the Manger Child
> Has brought God's life to me.

It was the right way to bring salvation to mankind.

But again we must make the personal application.

It is the right way only if we make it our way. To celebrate Christmas is not enough. Trees, carols, gifts and worship services are not enough, for Christmas is something that must be lived. What happened at Bethlehem is more than an event; it is a pattern for life. God said at Christmas that the way to win men is through love, through sacrifice and giving. And this is a pattern that must be constantly repeated. The children who dream of Christmas every day really know what life should be.

Unfortunately we are inclined to use other ways of dealing with our fellow men. The grandfather in the play wanted to throw his weight around. The children wanted to retaliate. But these are not the only methods that men use. Sometimes people seek to relate to others through bribery or wheedling. A number of years ago one of the best selling books was *How to Win Friends and Influence People,* in which all kinds of methods were suggested. Such a book has spawned a long line of successors all telling how to handle or manhandle our fellow men in this world.

But the method chosen by God is the right one. Love is the answer, and only love will really change men and enable them to live together in peace. Sometimes love seems as strange an idea as the sending of a baby in a manger to lift men out of their sin. Nevertheless love works. It breaks the hardest heart and redirects the most stubborn individual. It is the key, the solution to life on this earth.

We are always reluctant to come to the end of the Christmas season. We pack away the Christmas ornaments with a touch of sadness. "Another Christmas come and gone," we say. Yet one of our Christmas

hymns tells us how the spirit of Christmas can be
kept alive.

> O Holy Child of Bethlehem,
> Descend to us, we pray;
> Cast out our sin, and enter in,
> Be born in us today.
> We hear the Christmas angels
> The great glad tidings tell;
> O come to us, abide with us,
> Our Lord Immanuel.

DRAMA

The Star

MEDITATION

The Hopeful Minority

The Star

CHARACTERS

JOE *or* JOSEPH: young, idealistic, enthusiastic
DAVE *or* DAVID: fairly young, easily influenced
SAM *or* SAMUEL: a little older, wise, rather cynical
GEORGE: the custodian

SETTING

A room in a church. All that is needed is several chairs and a center area rather clear where most of the action takes place.

As the play opens, JOE, DAVE, *and* SAM *file onto the stage. They are dressed in black choir robes or similar costumes. They collapse onto the chairs. Their street clothes are hung on the chairs.*

111

JOE: Well, that's done for another year.

DAVE: Yeah. And we were good—as usual.

SAM: The hit of the show—with our three lines apiece.

JOE: At least we didn't forget our parts like King Herod did. Bill does that every time he plays that role. People will begin to think that Herod forgetting his lines is a part of the play. Bill's made the same mistake three years in a row. And he'll probably do it again next year.

DAVE: Do you think we'll have to do this silly play again next year?

JOE: Don't be naive. Of course we will.

SAM: Dave, you know the rich Mrs. Caswell wrote the play and the women of the church made the costumes. Two good reasons for repeating the performance year after year.

JOE *(mocking):* It's become a tradition in our church. Three years and we've got a tradition going.

SAM: Love those three-year traditions! Instant antiquity, the mark of our age.

DAVE: I suppose we're doomed to playing the scribes again next year, then. Once, just once I'd like to play one of the three kings and walk around in a fancy costume instead of this old choir robe. I'd even play the part of Herod if I had the chance. And I wouldn't forget the lines. I'll guarantee that.

JOE: Well, Dave, you study hard and work at your

part, and someday one of the kings will break a leg or Herod will get laryngitis, and your big moment will come.

SAM: Name up in lights and everything.

DAVE: All right, all right you guys. Guess there's no use worrying about a promotion. We're doomed to be the scribes who tell the wise men where to go, and that's that.

JOE: Yep, that's that. But you know, there's something in the play, in fact in the whole story that bothers me. It upsets me every time I play my part.

SAM: Are you being drama critic or Bible critic, Joe?

JOE: Maybe a little of both. You know, there's something in the story that doesn't ring true.

DAVE: What are you getting at?

JOE: Well, check me on my facts. Those scribes and all the rest of the Jews had been expecting a king, a Messiah, for a long while. Right?

SAM: Right!

JOE: O.K. So here come some guys, foreigners, in funny robes, and they want to know where the king of the Jews is to be born. Right?

SAM: You're batting a thousand so far. You must have listened to your Sunday school teacher more than I thought you did.

JOE: O.K., O.K. Now comes the problem. *(Slowly)* How come none of those scribes went down to

Bethlehem to see what was going on? How about it, eh?

DAVE: Say, that's right. I never thought of that. You'd have supposed they would jump at the chance.

SAM: There must be dozens of reasons, Joe, why they didn't go.

JOE: Maybe so. But I can't help wondering. Seems to me there must have been one of those scribes who said *(moves to center stage and becomes the Biblical character)*, Look fellows, what those men said in court today sounds like big news to me. A new king born in Bethlehem! We shouldn't let some odd foreigners be the ones to welcome him. Why don't we hurry down to Bethlehem and get there first. Of course the whole thing may be a fake but at least we ought to find out. How about it?

DAVE: I think you're right, Joe. There's a fellow like that in every crowd. And there's usually someone to agree with him. Like *(Moves toward center and becomes the biblical character too.)* That makes good sense, Joseph. We ought to go down right away. If we could be the first ones to discover the Messiah, people would be bound to notice us. We might even get a promotion and a raise in pay.

SAM: You're both right. There probably were scribes like that, even though the Bible doesn't mention them. But there's always someone in a crowd who throws cold water on a project. Such as—*(Same business as before. From this point on the three play the biblical parts until interrupted by* GEORGE.) When I listen to you two fellows it's not hard to see why you're both assistants and I'm the chief scribe.

JOE: What do you mean by that, Samuel?

SAM: Just let me ask you a simple question. Did either of you watch Herod's face when those magi or whatever they are were talking to him?

JOE: Watch Herod's face? Why should I? I've seen that evil leering look of his enough to last me a lifetime.

DAVE: Me too. The visitors were far more interesting with their gold-braided robes and the odd symbols on their sleeves. I particularly enjoyed watching the one with the long white beard.

SAM: I might have known. It's fun to look at a fellow with a long white beard, but you'll lose your neck doing it some day. *I* watched Herod's face.

JOE: So?

SAM: So—his lips were twisted into a half smile. The rest of his face was like a mask as if the soul within had gone on a journey. And his eyes blazed hatred. He couldn't completely hide the demon that dwells in him. I could read his mind as clearly as I could see the scroll in my hand. He was thinking, there is no place in this land for two kings, even if one of them is only a baby.

JOE: O Samuel, you're just imagining things.

SAM: Am I? Do you suppose the brute who killed his wife and his two sons because of jealousy and fear is going to shout hallelujah when someone tells him a rival has just been born in the land?

DAVE: But Herod seemed friendly. And he told those three men to come back and report to him so he can go and worship this king. That doesn't sound like he means to do anything wrong.

SAM: Oh stupidity, stupidity. Of course he told them to come back and report to him. That's the easiest way for him to learn who this new king really is. Herod doesn't want to alarm anyone by starting a search for a rival king. He doesn't want this child whisked out of the country to a safe place.

DAVE: Say, I never thought of that.

SAM: Of course you didn't, David. To repeat what I said at first, it's not hard to see why I'm the head scribe and you two are just assistants. And likely to remain so.

JOE *(angrily):* All right. So you think you're smart and clever. I still say we ought to go to Bethlehem and find this king. And if Herod isn't as friendly as he sounds, all the more reason for our trip. Someone ought to warn this young boy's parents about Herod.

DAVE: Yes. That's the right thing to do.

SAM: Oh sure, David. And what happens to us when Herod finds out that we three warned his rival to escape from him? And Herod will find out, never fear.

DAVE: Ugh. I can feel the sword in my back already.

JOE: David, David, you can blow hot and cold with the same breath. Don't be such a coward. Besides, we're servants of the High Priest. Herod wouldn't dare touch us.

SAM: I give up. Joseph, you sound like a greenhorn from Nazareth rather than a man who has lived in Jerusalem for twenty years. Do you honestly think the High Priest would protect us from Herod if Herod stirred up a fuss? We'd be three lambs delivered to the slaughter with an apology for our ever having existed. Protect us! Like a fox protects a chicken!

DAVE: You know, Joseph, I think Samuel's right. We'd better be careful.

JOE: No, he's not right. We're servants of God before everything else, and I intend to do what I think God wants me to do. If a new king has been born in this land, I'm his servant. Maybe I'll have to suffer for it, but I'll take my chances. I've had enough of Herod and his sly sinfulness.

SAM: Careful, Joseph. There are spies everywhere. So you mean to go to Bethlehem anyway, even if it gets the rest of us in trouble?

JOE: I don't intend to involve you two in anything. If Herod's men catch me, I'll insist that you refused to go to Bethlehem with me even when I coaxed you to go.

SAM: So we'll be tried for failure to report you! We lose our heads either way. Why, oh why, Joseph, can't you keep out of things that don't concern you?

JOE: This does concern me and every true Israelite. If God has finally sent us the Messiah, we've got to stand by him. You just can't say, let God do it all. Life has been sad and hopeless for Israel for a long while, what with Herod on the throne and the Roman power everywhere in the land. If there's a new king, a new beginning, then I'm ready to fight and die for my land and my people.

DAVE: You two men confuse me. I'm torn between fear and hope. I don't know which way to turn.

SAM: Well, to tell the truth, Joseph, you even confuse me a little bit. I don't like Herod any more than you do. But I happen to enjoy living, and life's pretty cheap to Herod. Look here. We've got a little time. It'll take those Magi several days to go to Bethlehem and return. We can watch Herod in the meantime. Maybe something will put him in a good mood and take his mind off this rival king. Maybe we won't have to worry about the safety of this child after all.

JOE: You're just playing for time, trying to make me postpone doing anything until it's too late.

SAM: Not really. But it never hurts to take a little time to study about a matter.

DAVE: Yes, Samuel's right, Joseph. Let's wait a little bit. It's foolish to act hastily.

JOE: But I . . . .

GEORGE *(walks in, seems amazed):* Say, are you three fellows still here? I'm getting ready to lock up the church. And you've still got your costumes on. What's going on here?

DAVE *(recovering first):* Oh, oh, it's all right, George. We were just—just talking.

GEORGE: Well, do your talkin' outside. *(Walks away muttering.)* Actors! *(Shakes head.)*

*(*JOSEPH *and* SAMUEL *now resume their former manner. They remove robes.)*

JOE: Say, that was queer. What came over us? It was almost as if we really were scribes back in that time.

SAM: Yeah. Talk about playing a part. Somehow we got carried away.

DAVE: Kinda spooky to me. It was just as if we were living in Herod's day. Thank goodness for the 20th century.

JOE: But now we'll never know how it all came out. Did that scribe Joseph go to Bethlehem or not?

SAM: Oh yes, we know the answer. He didn't go.

DAVE: How can you be so sure? Maybe the Bible just doesn't tell us that part.

SAM: I think we can be sure because people were no different then than they are now. Nobody wants to risk his neck for somebody else. And even the impetuous ones usually listen when someone says, "I think you're right. But let's not be hasty." Too little and too late. That's the verdict for the church.

JOE: Don't be so cynical.

SAM: How can I help it, when we've had Christianity for 1900 years and there's still poverty and hatred and prejudice and war in the world? Men never have listened to Jesus Christ, from his day until now. Last Sunday the preacher even read a text about it. How did it go? "He came unto his own and—and . . ."

DAVE: "His own received him not."

SAM: That's it. And people aren't doing any better now.

JOE: I'm not going to argue with you, Sam, as I did when I was a scribe in Jerusalem. I just want to remind you of those wise men. They came a long way to see this Jesus, and they weren't disappointed. And I still think some people today are led by that same star to Bethlehem and to their Savior.

DAVE: Yeah. The rest of that text you were quoting, Sam, says something about people who did receive Jesus and tells us that he gave them power to become sons of God. I believe that star in the east draws men today just as it did then. Things do get grim sometimes, but there are still some genuine followers of Jesus Christ in his church today.

SAM: Maybe you're right. God knows we need a star to lead us in this dark world.

GEORGE (*reappearing*): Say, are you three still here? I'm going to turn out the church lights in two minutes.

JOE: O.K., George. But we'll still have the star to guide us.

GEORGE: What?

JOE: Just dreaming again, just dreaming. Good night, guys.

DAVE: Goodnight.

SAM: Goodnight.

GEORGE: Goodnight!

The Hopeful Minority

Text: John 1:11-12

Christian people are sometimes too optimistic. Most of our associations are with our fellow Christians. We are a part of a culture that is permeated by Christian morals and influence. And so it is easy to get the notion that ours is the dominant faith in the world. It comes as a shock to learn that Christianity began as a minority religion, is still a minority religion, and probably will remain so as long as this world continues in its present form. Indeed, because of the rapid population increase in the so-called "non-Christian world," the percentage of believers in Christ is steadily declining.

This may seem a strange beginning to a sermon at Epiphany. Usually at this season we stress the public appearance of Jesus as the Messiah, and that is cause for great joy. Epiphany also has a missionary motif since it celebrates the coming of the Wise Men to Jesus, an event that indicated the gospel was for all people, not just for the Jews. A pessimistic message seems out of harmony with the events connected with Epiphany. Yet, unpleasant as it may seem to be, the minority status of the church must be faced. We Christians are hopelessly in the minority in this world.

Perhaps no verse of Scripture makes this truth plainer than the opening words of our text. "He came to his own and his own people received him not." These words have been labelled the saddest in the Bible. What a tragedy! For centuries the people of Israel had dreamed of a Redeemer, and yet when he appeared, he was rejected by the very people he came to save. The public ministry of Jesus bears out the truth of this verse. Jesus did receive some popular acclaim, yet his success was only a temporary thing. His followers deserted him, and at one time he was moved to ask his own disciples, "Will you also go away?" It is perhaps significant that in the parable of the sower Jesus described three kinds of soil that produced no harvest, and only the seed in the fourth soil proved productive. But perhaps the most crushing statement made by Jesus concerning the church as a minority was the declaration that only a few find the way that leads to eternal life. Certainly our Lord was under no illusions about the success of his gospel.

Let's face it. We are still a minority religion. Despite two thousand years of preaching and working, despite missionary endeavors and evangelistic campaigns, the majority of people are not enrolled in the Christian church. If success is measured solely by majorities, then our religion is a failure. Some of our difficulties have arisen because of the failure of the church to be true to its mission. Some of our slowness to win people for Christ has occurred because we must constantly begin again with each new generation. But most of the failure has the same cause as the sad message of our text: men simply do not receive the good news of the gospel.

Now of course we are not to resign ourselves to our minority status and let it go at that. But there are some important truths that can be drawn from this situation. For one thing, here is an answer to one of the accusations which the world frequently levels against the church. Men say, "We have had your gospel in the world for centuries. Yet look! We still have war and crime and poverty. Your faith is no good." Such logic is specious. No one can say how bad this world might be if the leaven of Christianity weren't in our midst. Besides, it is hardly fair to accuse the church of failure when it has never had the support of the majority of human beings. G. K. Chesterton once said, "Christianity has not been tried and found wanting; it has been found difficult and not tried." Those words are true for the majority of people. Jesus' own people didn't receive him and thus they lost the blessings which he brought. Men today in great numbers lost the comfort of Christ through their own rejection or indifference.

But there is another important truth that results from our minority status. We live in a democracy and are used to determining things by majorities. That is the proper way to decide the results of a political election. It is probably the proper way to determine the type of TV program to be broadcast: give the majority what they want—although one wonders at times about popular taste. But majorities are useless in determining matters of morals. You can't decide right and wrong by counting noses.

And this is an error that even Christians fall into at times. "Everybody's doing it," people say, and imply by those words that it must be the correct thing to do. The famous Kinsey report on sexual behavior was seized upon by many as an excuse for sexual license. If a certain percentage of people admit unfaithfulness to their marriage vows, then such action must be all right. This morality by majority is all wrong. Indeed, in matters of morals and of faith it is usually the minority who are right, although no such general rule can be adopted. But just as the majority were wrong in Jesus' day when they rejected him, so minorities are often far from the truth today.

Indeed, what the world needs desperately today are people who will stand for the right, regardless of the opinions of others. We need people who are concerned for the poor, regardless of the attitude of many toward the unfortunates in this world. We need people who will stand for honesty, regardless of how many people cheat on their income tax or engage in petty shoplifting. Since teenagers are particularly susceptible to the pressure of their peers, we need young men and young women who will resist pressure to take dope or to be sexually promiscuous simply because "everybody's doing it."

One of the great heroes of the faith is Joshua, the man who succeeded Moses as leader of the children of Israel. Joshua did not count noses to determine where public opinion was before making a decision. He simply said, "As for me and my house, we will serve the Lord." That's the true Christian spirit. It is the spirit which moved Jesus, hopelessly in the minor-

ity, to persist in his witness even though it finally
cost him his life. It is the spirit which we need today.
We dare not be afraid of our minority status. As
someone has said, "One man with God makes a
majority."

I began by saying that Christians are sometimes
too optimistic. At the same time we are often too
pessimistic. We too easily become a hopeless rather
than a hopeful minority. This happens when we think
there is no possibility for improvement. It seems easy
to get into a rut and stay there. We get the feeling
that life is bound to proceed in the same hopeless
routine with no chance for renewal or growth. "You
can't teach an old dog new tricks," we declare and
prepare to prove it by doing nothing. How often the
church seems to have no vision, no star to lead to
better things. One of the most devastating posters is
the one which says, "The Seven Last Words of the
Church: We Never Did It That Way Before."

In the midst of such pessimism we need to note
the second half of our text: "But to all who received
him, who believed in his name, he gave power to
become children of God." There is the message of
hope for us. We may not win everyone for the kingdom of God. Jesus didn't win all of his contempo-
raries either. But he did give men power to become
children of God and that power is still present in the
world today. We are to be a hopeful minority because
we know that God has and can change us through
Jesus Christ. God can give newness of life to all who
desire it in this world. The pessimist in our play did
not have the truth. The star still guides men who
are willing to follow.

That's why this text is a true Epiphany message.

It bears sad news, but it also announces good news. It reminds us that Jesus drew to his side a tax collector, a fallen woman, a thief, and many others who were transformed by his power. Much as we may lament that not all have believed, it is wrong to concentrate upon the failures of Christianity. That is like the minister who gazes at his congregation and thinks only about those who are not in church rather than those who have come. The Christian has cause to rejoice, cause to be hopeful for the future.

The evangelist Oral Roberts has attracted a sizeable following through his television broadcasts. I do not approve of all that he says and does. But he does catch the optimistic note of the second half of our text. He begins his broadcasts with the declaration: "Expect a miracle. Something good is going to happen to you." As a matter of fact, the Christian has already experienced a miracle for through the grace of God he has received power to become a son of God. Every believer is living proof of Christ's power. Let's be a *hopeful* minority in this world.